Contents

What Does It Mean to "Be an American"?

In my early years of teaching kindergarten, my class said the Pledge of Allegiance and sang a patriotic song each morning. At Thanksgiving we made our Pilgrim hats. On Presidents' Day the cotton-ball Washington-wig portraits went home. It all seemed very patriotic. But something was missing. Did my students really grasp what it meant to be an American? Not likely. Does a 5-year-old even have the capacity to understand?

Now, after a total curriculum makeover, I can emphatically answer *yes!* I have found that the best way for young children to fully appreciate America's remarkable spirit is to connect America's core values to their lives with minds-on, hands-on experiences. *Little Hands® Celebrate America!* is a guide to this discovery process.

What could be more compelling to a child than the story of America? It is through this story that our founding principles are revealed. Imagine people rejecting their king and inventing their own government — where "we the people" are the rulers. Here, children negotiate *A Kids' Bill of Rights*. Extending "liberty and justice for all" keeps America focused on its values. Children make a collage to celebrate this powerful pledge and to understand what we mean by *all* and how diversity enriches our lives.

At times America's actions have strayed from our founding principles, but in the end our ideals triumph. Freedom fosters an environment where courageous people can fight against injustice and win! Kids celebrate Martin Luther King Jr. Day by creating a *Brotherhood Chain*.

What happens when children hear our country's story and engage in these hands-on experiences? They discover a common American heritage, and they learn that although they are part of a community, as individuals they can make a crucial difference. And they begin to think profoundly and respond enthusiastically about being Americans!

America is about change and continuity. The 21st-century cities of our children's future will hardly resemble pioneer villages of the past. But the founding principles refined over more than 200 years will remain vibrant, enabling our children to succeed and our country to flourish. May the stories and activities in this book inspire your children to *Celebrate America!*

A Williamson  Book

LiTTLe HaNDs®

Learning about the U.S.A. through Crafts & Activities

BY JiLL FRaNKeL HaUSeR

iLLUSTRaTiONS BY MiCHaeL KLiNe

Williamson Books **W** Nashville, Tennessee

Published by Williamson Books
An imprint of Ideals Publications
A division of Guideposts
535 Metroplex Drive, Suite 250
Nashville, Tennessee 37211

Library of Congress Cataloging-in-Publication Data

Hauser, Jill Frankel, 1950-
    Little hands celebrate America! : learning about the U.S.A. through crafts & activities / Jill Frankel Hauser.
      p. cm. — (A Williamson Little Hands book)
    Summary: Easy crafts and activities like making crowns, Navajo bracelets, and a patchwork quilt, help introduce America's history, geography, symbols, and people.
    ISBN 1-885593-93-7
    1. United States—Juvenile literature. 2. Creative activities and seat work—Juvenile literature. 3. United States—Study and teaching (Preschool)—Activity programs. 4. United States—Study and teaching (Primary)—Activity programs. [1. United States. 2. Handicraft.] I. Title. II. Series.

E156.H385 2004
973—dc22
                                                            2003060786

Little Hands® series editor: **Susan Williamson**
Project editor: **Vicky Congdon**
Interior design: **Dana Pierson**
Interior illustrations: **Michael Kline**
Cover design and illustrations: **Michael Kline** and **Jon Kline**

10 9 8 7 6 5 4 3 2

Dedication

To my grandparents, David and Anna Frankel and Morris and Jennie Cohen, for their dreams, determination, and courage in coming to America!

Acknowledgments

Thank you, Rother School kindergartners. You have taught me so much about fairness and freedom, tolerance and pride, self-reliance and service. Our youngest Americans *do* have enormous hearts and profound minds!

Photography

page 18: Statue of Liberty, National Park Service; page 35: The Grand Canyon, National Park Service; page 38: Bryce Canyon National Park, National Park Service; page 39: Mesa Verde National Park, National Park Service; page 43: Mount Rushmore National Memorial, National Park Service; page 44: Washington Monument, National Park Service; page 45: Niagara Falls, © CORBIS Images; page 48: Hawaii Volcanoes National Park, © G. Brad Lewis Photography; page 50: Old Faithful, Yellowstone National Park, National Park Service; page 53: The Golden Gate Bridge, National Park Service; page 114: The Vietnam Veterans Memorial, National Park Service.

Keep Our Kids Safe!

Young children should always be supervised during a craft activity. Be wary of children putting objects in their mouths. Paper fasteners, safety pins, paper clips, and rubber bands can present choking and poking hazards. Decide when tools such as staplers or hole punches can be used safely. When scissors are used by a child, use only child safety scissors. Plastic bags can present a suffocation hazard. And bear in mind that even small amounts of water may pose a drowning risk to young children: Always supervise water play. Likewise, baking or the use of any sharp or pointed object should be done only by an adult.

We Say U.S.A.!

How do we say "U.S.A."? Wave our flag. Recite the Pledge of Allegiance. Display a picture of the Liberty Bell. These are all symbols of America. *Symbols* are cool because something simple, like a heart shape, can stand for something grand, like love. Our red, white, and blue flag stands for, or *symbolizes*, our entire country.

America is awesome because the ideas our country is built on are awesome. We use symbols, such as words, objects, and pictures, to stand for important ideas like freedom, fairness, equality, and self-rule. Each symbol says "U.S.A." in its own way. So the next time you spend a quarter, look at the image of George Washington, our first president, and think about the special way even it says "America."

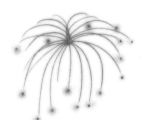

The United States Flag

What's the number one symbol of America? Close your eyes and picture the stars and stripes of our flag waving in the breeze. **Why those stripes?** Count them for a clue. There are 13, one for each of the original 13 colonies.

How about the stars? Count again. Stars were added for every new state, so there are 50.

And what about the colors? No one knows for sure, but most people think they stand for our values. *Values* are ideas we feel are so important that they shape the way we live our lives. Red is for *valor* — that means bravery. White is for *purity* (something that is pure is free of anything bad). And blue is for *justice*, or fairness.

Introducing ... the Flag!

Do you have a nickname? The American flag does. Old Glory, the Stars and Stripes, and the Star-Spangled Banner are all names for our flag!

My flag

★ ★ ★ ★ ★ ★

Make a flag that says you are proud to be an American!

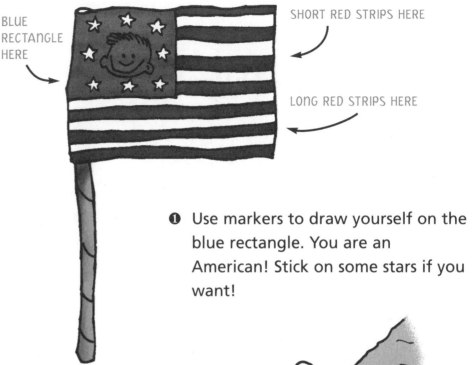

BLUE RECTANGLE HERE

SHORT RED STRIPS HERE

LONG RED STRIPS HERE

★ ★ You'll need ★ ★

Markers

Rectangle of blue paper, 4½" x 6"
    (11 x 15 cm)

Adhesive stars, optional

Glue

4 strips of red paper, ½" x 5"
    (1 x 10 cm)

3 strips of red paper, ½" x 11"
    (1 x 27.5 cm)

Sheet of white construction paper

Child safety scissors

Brown paper grocery bag

Drinking straw

❶ Use markers to draw yourself on the blue rectangle. You are an American! Stick on some stars if you want!

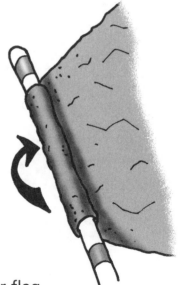

❷ Glue the blue rectangle and the red strips onto the white paper as shown on the finished flag.

❸ Now make the handle. Cut the front from the grocery bag. Starting from one corner, roll all the paper around the straw. Glue the edge to hold it together.

Glue the handle to the back of your flag.

Design Your Own Flag!

Imagine it's *your* job to create an American flag. Using only stars, stripes, and the colors red, white, and blue, paste up your own design. Cut your stars with one snip the Betsy Ross way (see Snip Snap Stars, page 106).

"Oh, Say Can You See ..."

Can a song be a symbol? Sure! **Francis Scott Key** wrote about his feelings when he saw the American flag still waving after a battle back in 1814. This wonderful poem became the words to "The Star-Spangled Banner," our *national anthem*, the official song of our country.

Here are the last two lines of that famous song:

Oh, say, does that star-spangled banner (a spectacular way to say a flag decorated with stars) *yet wave*

O'er (a poetic way to say "over") *the land of the free and the home of the brave?* (a powerful way to say U.S.A.)

Can you make up a song about our flag?

The Pledge of Allegiance

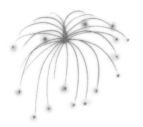
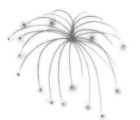

I pledge
(I promise)

allegiance
(to be faithful to)

to the flag of the United States of America,
(a symbol of our 50 states joined together as one great country)

and to the Republic for which it stands,
(our flag stands for a country where people pick their own leaders and make their own rules)

one nation under God,
(a place where everyone is important
and we come together as one country)

indivisible,
(we can't be divided)

with liberty
(with freedom to make good choices)

and justice
(having laws that make sure everyone is treated in an equal and fair way)

for all.
(for every American, including you and me!)

Pledge of Allegiance collage

★ ★ ★ ★ ★ ★ ★ ★ ★ ★ ★ ★ ★ ★ ★ ★ ★ ★ ★ ★

The **Pledge of Allegiance** was first said more than 100 years ago by millions of voices — including those of kids just like you! What a great way to start the school day or an important meeting. The more voices speaking together, the more powerful the pledge sounds!

Make a banner to celebrate this wonderful idea. A group of friends, a family, or an entire classroom of kids can work on this collage together!

★ ★ You'll need ★ ★

Marker

Map of the U.S.

Large sheet of paper (as large as you want your collage to be)

Old newspapers and magazines

Glue

Child safety scissors

❶ Have a grown-up help you draw an outline of the United States map on the paper.

❷ In the middle write the words: *With liberty and justice for all.*

❸ Cut out lots of pictures from the newspapers and magazines showing people living freely and fairly. Glue them inside the outline. Add your own drawings and photos. Don't forget to add a picture of guess who? You!

The Liberty Bell

Imagine your excitement! It's 1753 and you are eagerly waiting with a crowd to hear the first chime from Philadelphia's new bell. It came all the way from England — all 2,000 metal pounds (900 kg) of it! Then, *clank,* the bell cracks on the first strike! Two workers melt it down and recast it with copper. A few weeks later, you listen for the chime again. No one likes the tone of the new bell, however, so it's recast again, this time with tin.

Although the tone is still poor, the bell gets assigned history's most important chiming job. On July 8, 1776, thousands of people gather to hear the first public reading of the Declaration of Independence (page 22). The bell rings out to share its inscription, "Proclaim LIBERTY throughout all the Land unto all the Inhabitants thereof" (which means, let everyone know that we who live here are free).

Over the years, the **Liberty Bell** rang for many more important events. But while ringing for George Washington's birthday in 1846, it cracked beyond repair. Still, the bell was so famous and loved that it traveled around the country until people feared it would become more damaged. Now it is permanently on display in the Liberty Bell Center in Philadelphia, where it is gently tapped every Fourth of July!

Think about the Liberty Bell when you sing the last two lines of "My Country, 'Tis of Thee" (also known as "America"):

From ev'ry mountainside, let freedom ring.

Liberty Bell Pendant

★ ★ ★ ★ ★ ★ ★ ★ ★ ★ ★ ★ ★ ★ ★ ★

Proudly wear your bell on any patriotic holiday!

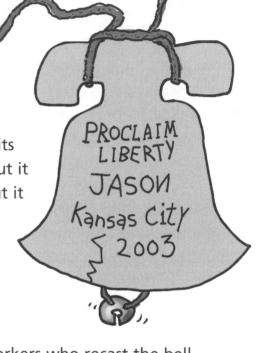

★ ★ You'll need ★ ★

Pencil

White paper

Child safety scissors

Thin cardboard

Fine-point black marker

Brown crayon (or copper, if you have it)

3' (1 m) of string or yarn

Small jingle bell

Tape

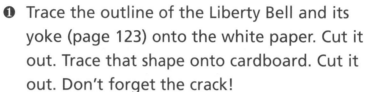

❶ Trace the outline of the Liberty Bell and its yoke (page 123) onto the white paper. Cut it out. Trace that shape onto cardboard. Cut it out. Don't forget the crack!

❷ Write these words on your bell with the marker so it's just like the real bell:

Proclaim LIBERTY (part of the quotation on the real bell)

Your name (just like the names of the workers who recast the bell, John Pass and John Stow)

Your town (just like Philadelphia)

Today's date (the letters MDCCLIII on the real bell are Roman numerals that mean the year 1753)

Lightly color your bell.

❸ Thread a short piece of string through the jingle bell and tape it to the back. Loop the remaining string around the bell's yoke. Knot the ends.

The Science of Sound

What broke the Liberty Bell? The same powerful *vibrations* (back-and-forth movements) that make it ring. Strike a bell and the tiny particles that make up the metal *vibrate* (move). Those vibrations move the air back and forth as they travel to your ear. You hear that movement as *bong!*, a bell ringing.

You can experiment with creating the best bell chime just as Pass and Stow, the Liberty Bell makers, did.

❶ Tie the hook of a hanger at the center of about 3' (1 m) of string. Wrap the ends of the string around your index fingers. Place your fingertips in each ear.

❷ Lean over and swing the hanger so that it taps against a table. *BONG!*

Here are some ways to experiment:

★ Listen to the same sound without placing your fingertips in your ears.

★ Vary the length of the string.

★ Tie a spoon or empty tin can to the string.

Which way do you think makes the best chime?

The American Bald Eagle

Why is the **bald eagle** a symbol of our freedom-loving country? Imagine the life of an eagle and you'll see why we've chosen it as our national bird. This majestic bird swoops from lofty mountaintops into valleys below. It is so strong and powerful that it seems to live in total freedom.

Find the eagle on a dollar bill. It's also on the gold dollar, on some versions of the silver dollar, and on the Presidential Seal. Notice its *talons,* or claws. In the left it holds arrows, a symbol of strength. In the right it holds an olive branch, a symbol of peace. What does this say about America? We strive to be a strong and peaceful nation.

And here's more symbolism! The eagle holds 13 arrows. The olive branch has 13 leaves. What's so special about this number? The 13 original colonies became the first 13 states!

Balancing Bird

★ ★ ★ ★ ★ ★ ★ ★ ★ ★ ★ ★

Make an eagle that *symbolizes* balancing strength and peace. It even balances on your fingertip!

★ ★ **You'll need** ★ ★

Pencil

Sheet of white paper

Child safety scissors

Thin cardboard

Glue

Brown crayon

Markers

Tape

2 pennies

❶ Trace the eagle pattern on page 124 two times onto white paper. Cut each eagle out. Trace one eagle onto the cardboard. Cut it out.

❷ Glue the three shapes together with the cardboard one in the middle.

❸ Lightly color the eagle brown, leaving the head and tail feathers white. Decorate the top side to look like the front of an eagle.

Draw the eagle's talons on one side. Draw an olive branch in one talon and arrows in the other.

❹ Tape pennies at each wing tip. Bend the beak and balance the bird on your fingertip.

Eagle Facts

★ Eagles were important to Native Americans. They decorated shields and headdresses with the feathers. Eagle feathers were a symbol of power and speed. Can you see why?

★ The eagle is not really bald. It has white feathers on its head. To the colonists, bald meant white, not hairless.

★ Not everyone thought the eagle should be the national bird. Benjamin Franklin (one of the signers of the Declaration of Independence, page 22) thought it should be the turkey! Take a survey of friends and family. Which bird do they think would be best?

★ Long ago Americans thought the bald eagle only lived in America. This isn't true, but today, half of the world's eagles do live in Alaska.

★ The eagle's worst enemy is pollution, which destroys its *habitat* (home) so it cannot live. The eagle has been *endangered*, which means it might disappear forever. Imagine America without eagles! Today eagles are *threatened*. That means more are surviving, but we still must help the eagle and protect it.

Collect State Quarters!

For many years, the eagle was on the back of the quarter. It's temporarily been replaced by a special set of quarters honoring all 50 states. These quarters are being released over the next few years in the order that each state became part of the United States.

Lots of kids are collecting these state quarters. Is your state quarter out yet? Check the website of the U.S. Mint at ‹**www.usmint.gov**› to find out!

A "Hand-Some" Eagle!

Place both hands on a piece of paper with your thumbs side by side to form an eagle body and head. Stretch out your fingers to form wings. Have a friend trace around your hands along the tips of your fingers. Add a tail, and presto, you've got an eagle!

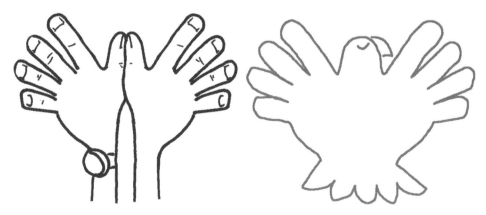

The Statue of Liberty

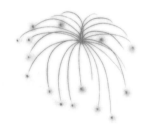

Imagine receiving a colossal 450,000-pound (202,500-kg) metal woman for your birthday! That's exactly what France gave America in 1886. Even more awesome than the **Statue of Liberty**'s size is her message of hope and welcome to America's newcomers. She stands in New York Harbor with her torch of freedom shining for people all over the world. The statue's original name was *Liberty Enlightening the World.* Can you see why?

Crown and Torch

★ ★ ★ ★ ★ ★ ★ ★ ★ ★ ★ ★ ★ ★ ★ ★ ★

Drape a green sheet over your shoulder and dress up freedom-style!

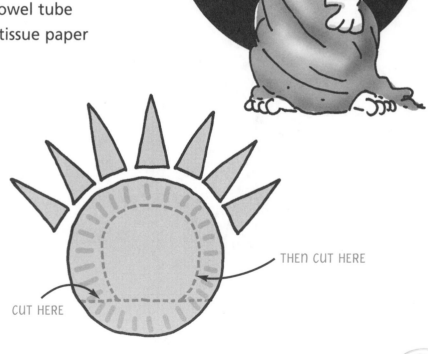

★ ★ You'll need ★ ★

Child safety scissors

Ruler

Paper plate

Green tempera paint and paintbrush

Green construction paper

Glue

Paper-towel tube

Yellow tissue paper

Crown of Continents

❶ Cut about 3" (7.5 cm) off the bottom of a paper plate. Cut out the center, leaving about a 2" (5 cm) headband. Adjust to fit your head snugly. Paint both sides green.

❷ Cut seven green-paper triangles, each with a 2" (5 cm) base and 6" (15 cm) high. These are the rays, one for each continent. Glue them evenly in place across the headband.

THEN CUT HERE

CUT HERE

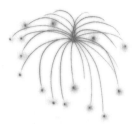

Torch of Freedom

❶ Paint the tube green.

❷ Stuff it with yellow tissue paper to look like a flame.

Why Green?

The Statue of Liberty is covered with a thin layer of copper, the same metal used for pennies.

Try this experiment to see what happens when copper is exposed to the "pollution" of vinegar.

❶ Fold a paper towel to fit the bottom of a plastic bowl.

❷ Soak it in vinegar.

❸ Place pennies on top.

❹ Notice how the pennies change after several hours.

Did you discover how the Statue of Liberty turned green? Check below to see if you are right!

Why Green? *Pollution in the air causes "acid rain," which reacts with copper to form a green coating on the statue. Vinegar is an acid, too, so it turns the copper pennies green.*

Welcome to America!

Emma Lazarus wrote this poem called "The New Colossus" (a *colossus* is a gigantic statue). It appears on the pedestal beneath Lady Liberty (her nickname!). The last few lines are so famous, many Americans can recite them from memory!

Give me your tired, your poor,

Your huddled masses yearning to breathe free,

The wretched refuse of your teeming shore;

Send these, the homeless, tempest-tost to me,

I lift my lamp beside the golden door!

The message? Even if you are poor or unwelcome in your own country, you are welcome in America if you long to be free!

Just How Colossal?

★ There are 354 steps inside the statue leading to the Statue of Liberty's crown. Count them off across your playground or sidewalk. Make chalk lines to show the first and last steps. Your friends can help step and count up to the total.

★ Her nose is $4\frac{1}{2}'$ (1.35 m) long. Is that longer or shorter than your height?

★ If you were buying sandals for Lady Liberty, you'd need to search for a size 250! That's what it would take to fit her 25' (7.5 m) foot!

The Declaration of Independence

We hold these truths to be self-evident,
that all men are created equal,
that they are endowed by their Creator
with certain unalienable Rights,
that among these are
Life, Liberty, and the pursuit of Happiness.

These famous words mean that *all* Americans have the same right to:

> *Life* (living),
>
> *Liberty* (freedom),
>
> *and the pursuit of Happiness* (being able to do what makes you happy!)

For yourself and for everyone!

These powerful ideas come from the **Declaration of Independence**. It's an announce- ment (a *declaration*) from more than 200 years ago that we would no longer be part of England (that's *independence*). What a courageous statement! We let the world know that we were creating a new nation where people would live in freedom. Fifty-six people signed the declaration to say, "We agree!" with this basic American ideal. John Hancock proudly wrote his name largest of all.

My Declaration

★ ★ ★ ★ ★ ★ ★ ★ ★ ★ ★ ★ ★ ★

Write a declaration of what's important to you. Draw a picture to explain your idea. Write the date at the top.
July 4, 1776, is the date you'll *see* on the Declaration of Independence. Sign your name at the bottom, boldly and proudly, just like John Hancock!

Here are some *virtues* (the good ways we think and act to make America a wonderful place) you might like to declare:

★ We must take care of the earth.

★ We should help others be happy.

★ We should take turns.

★ We must be kind and fair.

★ We should have time to play.

We resolve that all animals are created equal, and that we should recycle as much as possible.

Your Super Signature!

The way you sign your name is your own style. It's called your *signature*. Here are some special signature styles.

★ Rainbow-write by outlining the letters with several colors.

★ Make a fancy decoration beneath or on top of your name.

★ Add tiny decorations at the tops of lines or inside circles of letters.

★ Add a second dotted or dashed line around each letter.

★ Use a different color for each letter.

It's All-American!

Signing the Declaration of Independence took courage, one of the virtues that makes America and its people great. Our history is full of stories of brave people and their actions. Throughout this book you find lots of examples, along with other virtues such as compassion, imagination, self-reliance, determination, and tolerance that all define what it is to be an American! See how many you can find. Here are a few to get you started.

The Constitution of the United States

We, the people of the United States ...

The **Constitution of the United States** begins with these remarkable words. After all, it was the first time ordinary people had created the rules to start a new nation. Writing the Constitution was hard work, and it took imagination and creativity. So many people had to agree to so many new ideas. There was lots of discussion and *compromise* (I'll agree to this if you agree to that!). In the end, a powerful document was created that we still live by today. At its heart is the belief that we Americans enjoy rights equally and that we rule ourselves!

Election Button

★ ★ ★ ★ ★ ★ ★ ★ ★ ★ ★ ★ ★ ★

How do we Americans pick our leaders and rules? The Constitution says that each citizen gets a vote! We share our ideas and try to convince others to agree with us. Of course, the wonderful thing about America is that each of us can vote as we please.

Make a button to show everyone one of your important ideas about how to make America a better place!

★ ★ You'll need ★ ★

Pencil	Tape
Can or plastic cup	Safety pin
Thin cardboard	Strips of colored paper
Child safety scissors	Glue
Markers	

❶ Trace around the can or cup on the cardboard. Cut out the circle.

❷ Write or draw your slogan on the circle.

❸ Tape the pin to the back.

❹ Glue the strips around the button as a decoration.

Get Out the Vote!

You can make bumper stickers or posters to share your ideas for America. Write or draw your ideas on paper. A computer or copy machine helps you make many copies. Tape slogans to walls or in windows.

- ★ Build Playgrounds Now!
- ★ Our Town Needs a Pool

- ★ Protect Our Forests
- ★ Be Kind to Animals
- ★ Don't Litter
- ★ Jason for President
- ★ More $ for Schools
- ★ VOTE!

HONK IF YOU RECYCLE

— HONK!

Thank you, Susan B.

Can you imagine being arrested for voting? That's just what happened to **Susan B. Anthony**. It was against the law for her to vote just because she was a woman! Anthony said this was unfair, especially in a country that believed in equality and self-rule. She never gave up her courageous fight for the right of women to vote. She wrote books, gave speeches, and led groups. She died before her dream came true. Thanks to the hard work of Anthony and others, a new law was added to the Constitution. Now women can vote! Look for her on the front of our silver dollar coin.

The Bill of Rights

When a law is added to the Constitution, it's called an *amendment*. The first 10 amendments to the Constitution are so important, they have a special name: the **Bill of Rights** (here, the word *bill* means a list). This special part of our Constitution promises precious, powerful freedoms that can never be taken away from any American.

Freedom of Religion
(we can believe what we want to believe)

Freedom of Assembly
(we can peacefully meet in a group)

Freedom of Speech
(we can talk about our ideas even if they are unpopular or others disagree with them)

Freedom of the Press
(we can share our ideas through newspapers, magazines, websites, and television and radio shows)

Hot off the Press!

★ ★ ★ ★ ★ ★ ★ ★ ★ ★ ★ ★ ★ ★ ★ ★

Celebrate freedom of the press kid-style by making your own newspaper. Invite your friends to be reporters and join in the fun. Then invite folks to read the latest news!

★ ★ You'll need ★ ★

Paper
Pencil
Crayons
Camera, optional
Child safety scissors
Glue
Old newspaper

❶ Write stories about what's happening in your neighborhood or school. You can write about yourself, your family, or your friends. Draw pictures or take photos. Write on paper (or use a computer). Be sure to add your own headlines, give weather reports, and tell about sports and special events. Do it your way!

❷ Glue your stories onto the pages of a real newspaper.

EXTRA!
EXTRA!

Kid News

Yesterday we went to the park and s[...] a dog. It [...] funny.

SPORTS

Our team won yesterday!!

More Freedom Fun!

Kid of the Year!

Glue your picture on the cover of an old news magazine. Glue stories about yourself inside.

TV Reviewer

Write or draw pictures about cool and not-so-cool television shows. Tell why you think so. Glue them into an old TV program guide.

Sports Reporter

Write and draw pictures about sports that you and your friends enjoy watching or playing. Glue them inside an old sports magazine.

A Kids' Bill of Rights

Meet with a group of friends to create your own Kids' Bill of Rights. Are there 10 ideas you can all agree on? Are they fair to everyone?

Here are some ideas other kids have had. Do you agree with them?

Kids have the right to:

★ be loved and respected

★ choose what they like or don't like

★ be safe and protected

★ go to bed when they please

★ ask questions

★ wear the clothes they choose

★ agree and disagree with others

★ be alone or with others

★ pick their own friends

★ eat only the foods they like

The White House

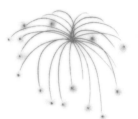

NOW WHERE DID I PUT THAT WHITE PAINT?

When the United States was still a new country, most other countries were ruled by kings and queens. They became rulers just because they had been born into a certain family. They could make people follow whatever rules they wanted. We Americans decided to do things quite differently.

We would still have a leader, but we would pick or elect him because of his ideas, not his family. And he wouldn't live in a palace. He'd live in "our house." The **White House** is where every president since John Adams (the second U.S. president) has lived.

Keep-Track Plaque

* * * * * * * * * * * * * * *

We keep track of important events that happen at the White House. In fact, there's a stone plaque at its entrance engraved with dates of events such as when the building was started and when the West Wing was added. Make a plaque to honor the important events at your home.

❶ Open the flap of the envelope. Decorate the envelope with markers to look like a house with the flap as a roof. Write your family's name and address across the roof line.

❷ On each paper strip, write, draw, and date an important event about your home. Store the cut strips inside the envelope.

HERE ARE SOME IDEAS. The day ...

We moved into our house.
My sister was born.
I got a new bike.

 You'll need * *

Legal-size envelope
Markers
3 sheets of paper, cut into thirds

What a great way to celebrate important times in your home!

What's the Most Famous Address in America?

1600 Pennsylvania Avenue
Washington, D.C. 20500

Dear Mr. President,
My dad says I can't
watch TV until I
eat my carrots.
Would you call him
please?

　　　　—mikey

That's the address of the White House!

The White House is America's house, because so many important decisions about our nation are made within its walls. You can be a part of those decisions by sharing your ideas with the president. How? Just write a letter to the president at that address! Share your idea with words and drawings. Be sure to include your own address. Then watch your mailbox. You'll get a letter back from — you guessed it! — the White House!

★ ★

Madam President!

So far, all the U.S. presidents have been men. But there's no law that says it has to be that way! Wouldn't it be exciting to see that change? Now *that* would be an event to add to that plaque at the White House!

★ ★

From Sea to Shining Sea!

O beautiful for spacious skies,
For amber waves of grain,
For purple mountain majesties
Above the fruited plain!
America, America!
God shed his grace on thee
And crown thy good with
        brotherhood
From sea to shining sea!

America *is* beautiful! That's what Katharine Lee Bates thought in 1893 as she gazed out at the spectacular view from the top of Pikes Peak, Colorado. Then she wrote the poem "America the Beautiful" that we sing today.

America is filled with treasures – our national parks, monuments, and memorials. Some we love because they are wonders of nature. Others we love because they show what Americans have accomplished. We protect these special places for all people to enjoy forever – Americans and visitors from around the world, you, your friends and family, and someday, even your children!

The Grand Canyon

What does it take to make the world's grandest canyon? Muck! It's hard to imagine, but long, long ago, a sea covered the desert of the western United States. Tons of powdery rock and sand, called *silt*, was in the water. The silt sank to the bottom, and the ocean dried up, leaving a thick, mucky layer behind. Over millions of years, many seas were there and then dried up. They left more mucky layers of silt, one on top of the other. As the layers dried, and their weight pressed down on the others, they hardened into rock.

Can you believe that running water could be powerful enough to cut through all those rock layers? Well, 6 million years ago, the Colorado River began *eroding*, or rubbing away, the rock as the river flowed along. Over time, it cut a deep groove, or *canyon*, down through the different types of rock. That's why you see so many colorful rock layers in the canyon walls when you visit **Grand Canyon National Park** in northern Arizona. The river still flows through the canyon floor. It keeps eroding and changing the canyon, making it even grander!

Create a Mini-Canyon!

★ ★ ★ ★ ★ ★ ★ ★ ★ ★ ★ ★ ★ ★ ★ ★ ★ ★ ★

Admire the *beautiful* layers of your canyon walls.
Then eat them!

★ ★ You'll need ★ ★

Table knife
Peanut butter
3 slices of bread
Jam or honey

Raisins
Bananas
Plate

rrp!

❶ To form your edible rock layers, spread peanut butter on a slice of bread. Now add a layer of jam or honey, then raisins. Top with another slice of bread.

Next add layers of peanut butter, jam or honey, and thinly sliced bananas. Top with the last slice of bread.

❷ "Erode" the "land" by cutting a jagged path through the sandwich. Your knife is doing the work of the Colorado River!

A Really *Grand* Canyon!

If you love enormous numbers, then the Grand Canyon is your kind of place. After all, it's the world's largest canyon!

★ It covers more than 1 million acres of land (405,000 hectares). That's about 900,000 football fields.

★ Ask a grown-up to you show you a place one mile (1.6 km) from your home. Now imagine traveling *down* that same distance. The canyon is that deep in some places!

★ It's 277 miles (446 km) long and as much as 18 miles (29 km) across.

★ Some rocks are 2 billion years old. That's before the dinosaurs lived!

★ More than 5 million tourists visit each year. Will you be one of them?

Silty Science

Shake up some soil, sand, and water in a jar. Now let your "ocean" cover part of planet Earth by pouring it into a pie plate. Let your ocean dry for "a few million years" by leaving the plate in the sun for a while. Does the silt sink to the bottom and form a layer?

"Hoodoo" You Look Like?

Maybe a boat, a castle, or even a wild animal! If you were a rock shape at **Bryce Canyon National Park** in Utah, that is! Water and ice have done weird work on these canyon layers. Some rock layers are softer than others, so they wear away in different ways. They form columns in a variety of fantastic shapes called *hoodoos*. Layers of red, pink, copper, and tan change in the sunlight. Look at this photo from Bryce Canyon — what do you think you see?

The Cliff Dwellings of Mesa Verde

Imagine the steep walls of a desert canyon. Now picture tall apartment buildings clinging to those cliffs. That's just what the ancient dwellings of Mesa Verde look like. Can you see people bustling along through the streets and in the gathering places? They are the *Anasazi*, who built these amazing cliff cities 800 years ago.

You can visit these dwellings today at **Mesa Verde National Park** in Colorado. **Square Tower House** was an 80-room building, several stories high. **Long House** was built beneath an overhanging cliff. Its large central *plaza* (open space) and great *kiva* (room for ceremonies) were probably used for special gatherings. **Cliff Palace** was a entire village, set on a mountain ledge. With more than 200 rooms and four-story walls, it was home to as many as 250 people at one time!

So why would the Anasazi suddenly vanish from their magnificent cities? Maybe you can solve that mystery as you explore Mesa Verde.

Be a Potter

★ ★ ★ ★ ★ ★ ★ ★ ★ ★

The Anasazi were not only awesome builders, they were wonderful potters, too! Women made pots, bowls, mugs, jars, and ladles from clay. Mothers passed down designs to their daughters. Try making their black-on-white designs on your own pot.

★ ★ You'll need ★ ★

Salt dough (see below)
Black marker

❶ Form a bowl shape with the dough. Let the bowl dry.

❷ Decorate your bowl with the marker. Make striped, zigzag, and checker patterns like the Anasazi.

Salt Dough

2 cups (500 ml) flour
1 cup (250 ml) salt
3/4 to 1 cup (175 to 250 ml) water
2 tablespoons (30 ml) vegetable oil

In a bowl, mix together the flour and salt. Slowly add the water and the oil to the flour mix. Stir until a dough forms.

Be an Archaeologist

Archaeologists are science detectives who figure out how ancient people may have lived. They search for clues in what's left of the stuff people used long ago. Tools, dwellings, cloth, bones, bits of pottery, drawings, and more can all hold secrets to the past.

It's strange but helpful that the Anasazi left their buildings and belongings behind. They also tossed scraps of food, broken dishes, and tools into their front-yard canyon.

Here's what we know ...

Garbage heaps, buildings, bones, and belongings tell stories of the Anasazi's daily lives:

★ Short doorways tell us people weren't as tall as they are today.

★ The age of the bones found tell us they did not live as long as people do today.

★ Blackened walls tell of keeping warm by fires during cold winters.

★ Pitch-lined baskets tell how water was carried and boiled.

★ Yucca-fiber sandals, turkey-feather robes, and dog-hair sashes tell how they dressed and depended on nature to clothe themselves.

Here's what we don't know ...

There are still big mysteries to solve:

★ Why did the Anasazi build their homes into cliffs? Didn't it make getting around difficult and dangerous?

★ Why did they vanish? Was there a *drought* (no rain for crops)?

★ Why did they leave their belongings behind? Was an enemy about to attack?

What does your stuff say about you?

Pretend you are an archaeologist in the future, guessing what life was like for an American family of our time. Here's what you have unearthed from their garbage. Can you answer these questions?

★ Soup can, apple core, candy wrapper, soda can. *How did these people eat?*

★ CD, TV program listing, broken toy. *What did they do for fun?*

★ Cell phone, computer, letters, pencil. *How did they communicate?*

★ Jacket, blanket, heater. *How did they stay warm?*

★ Car tire, skateboard, subway ticket. *How did they travel?*

Mount Rushmore

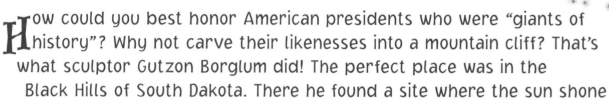

GEORGE WASHINGTON

How could you best honor American presidents who were "giants of history"? Why not carve their likenesses into a mountain cliff? That's what sculptor Gutzon Borglum did! The perfect place was in the Black Hills of South Dakota. There he found a site where the sun shone for much of the day and the granite was soft and grainy. "Here is the place!" Borglum said. "American history shall march along that skyline."

THOMAS JEFFERSON

Whose faces would be carved? Presidents whose ideas were as big and bold as the monument!

THEODORE ROOSEVELT

George Washington stands for our fight to become a new nation. **Thomas Jefferson** stands for the idea that we are a nation of people who rule ourselves.

ABRAHAM LINCOLN

Theodore Roosevelt stands for our country's place in the world.

Abraham Lincoln stands for equality among people and unity of our states. These four massive faces at the **Mount Rushmore National Memorial** seem to look out across America.

A Tall, Proud Monument

★ ★ ★ ★ ★ ★ ★ ★ ★ ★ ★ ★ ★ ★ ★ ★ ★ ★ ★

Rising to a height of 555' (171 m) is the world's tallest stone tower, the **Washington Monument** in our nation's capital, Washington, D.C. It doesn't look a bit like George Washington, but it still honors him! Monuments can be built in the spirit of people's ideas or actions, not just in their images.

Make a monument out of salt dough (page 40) for a friend or family member. Mold your dough into a shape that says, "You're great!"

Niagara Falls

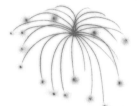

See water gush at up to 36 million gallons (133 million L) per minute. Think about just one gallon (3.7 L) of milk!

Hear water thunder as it crashes 170' (52 m) from the crest line above to the river below. Imagine five school buses stacked end to end.

Feel the drenching spray as you stand on "Hurricane Deck" at Cave of the Winds.

This is what it's like to visit **Niagara Falls State Park** in western New York!

What created one of the world's most awesome waterfalls? Ice and an ocean bottom! Millions of years ago an ocean dried up. The edge of its ancient floor formed a rocky cliff. Then, 12,000 years ago, melting ice caused Lake Erie to overflow. The overflow became the Niagara River, flowing north between New York and Canada to Lake Ontario. The raging river plunged over that rocky cliff and presto! (well, not quite) — spectacular Niagara Falls!

Make a Mini-Falls

★ ★ ★ ★ ★ ★ ★ ★ ★ ★ ★ ★ ★ ★ ★

See for yourself how gravity creates a waterfall.

★ ★ You'll need ★ ★

Scissors (for grown-up use)
Empty gallon (3.7 L) milk or juice carton
Garden hose or faucet

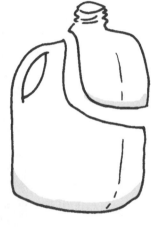

❶ Ask a grown-up to cut the carton as shown.

❷ Set the carton on the ground in your backyard or in a sink. Turn on the hose or faucet so that water flows gently into the carton. That's your river!

What happens when the water overflows? It falls over the low edge, forming a curtain of water. There's your mini-Niagara!

It's All about Gravity!

Did you ever think about what happens when you drop something? It always falls to the ground. That's because everything — even water — is pulled to the center of the earth by *gravity*. This invisible force makes water flow to the lowest point around. Sometimes water gets stuck behind rocks or earth and forms a lake. Otherwise, it's on the move, flowing down until it reaches the ocean. Niagara Falls is a spectacular show of gravity's pull on water!

★ "Friendship Falls" would be a great nickname for Niagara Falls. After all, the longest, friendliest international border, between the United States and Canada, runs right through the middle of it.

★ The three falls of Niagara are **American** (or **Rainbow**), **Bridal Veil**, and **Horseshoe** (on the Canadian side).

★ Since 1901, 15 daredevils have tried to go over the falls in crazy containers. (Ten lived.) The first person, a 63-year-old school teacher from Michigan, went over in a wooden barrel! There is a $10,000 fine for trying to go over the falls.

★ 14 million people visit Niagara Falls each year. Will you be one?

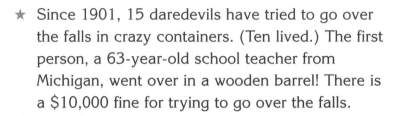

Tallest Falls!

It hasn't got the huge flow of Niagara, but these falls are 14 times the height! If you love tall, then head for **Yosemite National Park** in California. The park's steep cliffs and low valley make it home to spectacular waterfalls. Yosemite Falls drops almost half a mile from crest to valley floor. That makes it America's tallest falls!

Hawaii Volcanoes National Park

Think Hawaii, and you'll think of *volcanoes!* Our 50th state was created millions of years ago from volcanoes deep on the ocean floor. When you visit **Hawaii Volcanoes National Park**, you can watch the island of Hawaii continue to grow. Lava flowing from Kilauea (kee-law-WAY-ah)— the world's most active volcano — actually builds new land right before your eyes! Mauna Loa, the world's biggest active volcano, is the largest mountain on earth!

THIS ERUPTION IS TYPICAL OF THE SIGHTS YOU'LL SEE AT HAWAII VOLCANOES NATIONAL PARK.

Luscious Lava

★ ★ ★ ★ ★ ★ ★ ★ ★ ★ ★ ★ ★ ★

Explore different types of lava when you create this volcanic ice-cream treat with some friends. Then dig in!

★ ★ You'll need ★ ★

½ gallon (2 L) of ice cream,
    slightly softened
Large plate
Table knife and spoon
Chocolate chips
Microwave-proof bowl
Chocolate cookie crumbs
Chocolate sprinkles

Make the volcano

Turn the container onto the plate and peel away the carton. Shape the ice cream into a mountain peak.

Make the lava

❶ *Lava* is formed when *magma* (melted rock deep inside the earth) erupts from a volcano. Ask a grown-up to melt some chocolate chip "rocks" in the microwave. Dribble the "lava" over the peak of the volcano and down the sides.

❷ *Pumice* is lava thrown into the air during an eruption. It falls to the ground as rock. Trapped gas bubbles makes it very light. Crumble chocolate cookies around the volcano to make pumice.

❸ *Black sand* is formed when hot lava hits the ocean and breaks into tiny grains. Add chocolate sprinkles to the base of the volcano.

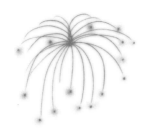

Old Faithful

Imagine some 8,400 gallons (31,080 L) of boiling water exploding 150' (46 m) into the air almost every hour! That's the geyser known as Old Faithful. Watch the action at **Yellowstone National Park**, America's first national park, located in Idaho, Montana, and Wyoming. If you get tired of Old Faithful's sky-high blast, you've still got more than 2 million acres (810,000 h) of wilderness to explore! Enjoy the abundant wildlife, or stick to the watery wonders of the land.

Geyser Gizmo

⭐ ⭐ ⭐ ⭐ ⭐ ⭐ ⭐ ⭐ ⭐ ⭐ ⭐

Gas bubbles are powerful. Old Faithful erupts when underground bubbles of steam push water out of cracks in the earth. Your gizmo erupts when *bubbles* from your breath push water out the tip of the funnel. It's a bubbly blast!

⭐ ⭐ You'll need ⭐ ⭐

Funnel
Bowl or pot
Flexible straw
Small stones

❶ Set the funnel on the bottom of the bowl or pot, wide-end down.

❷ Place the flexible end of the straw under the funnel rim. Hold the funnel down with the stones.

❸ Fill the bowl or pot with water up to the funnel stem.

❹ Blow through the free end of the straw. Your geyser erupts!

Fizz, Bubble, and Splat!

Yellowstone has more geysers, hot springs, and mud pots than in all the rest of the world combined.

Geyser. *Stand back!* When underground water hits hot rocks, it boils, turns to steam, and explodes into the air through whatever opening it can find.

Mud pot. *Gurgle, hiss, splat!* Gas from inside the earth bubbles up through soupy mud. Picture an enormous pot of simmering oatmeal and you'll get the idea of a mud pot.

Hot springs. *No swimming allowed!* Hot water from underground rises to the surface and forms pools. Some are boiling hot! Many are very colorful.

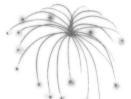

The Golden Gate Bridge

When is a bridge more than a structure that takes you from here to there? When it's also a symbol (page 5) for hope and freedom! Just like the Statue of Liberty (page 18), the **Golden Gate Bridge** welcomes newcomers to America.

Find New York City on a map of the United States. That's where Lady Liberty greets folks traveling across the Atlantic Ocean. Now move your hand west across the entire country. There's San Francisco. That's where the Golden Gate Bridge greets folks coming to America from across the Pacific Ocean. What countries might they be from?

Grab a jacket. Brave the ocean winds and dense fog. And walk almost two miles (3.2 km) across the great Golden Gate!

Bridge It!

★ ★ ★ ★ ★ ★ ★ ★ ★

A *suspension* (hanging) bridge like the Golden Gate *spans* (reaches across) a long distance. Even though it is very strong, it doesn't use a lot of construction materials. Here's an easy-to-make suspension bridge that will support a toy car!

★ ★ You'll need ★ ★

6' (2 m) of string
2 full quart (1 L) bottles
Ruler
3" x 8" (7.5 x 20 cm) strip of cardboard
Toy car

❶ Tie the ends of the string together to make a large loop. Set the bottles on the floor and loop the string around the necks. Move the bottles apart until the string hangs about 3" (7.5 cm) above the floor.

❷ Bend both long edges of the cardboard down about ½" (1 cm). Set this roadway over the string cables. Will it hold your car? You just made a lightweight but strong suspension bridge!

The Gateway Arch

Imagine your pioneer family is about to travel to a new home. Behind you is St. Louis, the last post for buying supplies for your long trip west. Before you lies unknown wilderness. America's tallest national monument marks this special spot.

Like the Golden Gate Bridge (page 53), the **Gateway Arch** was a tricky structure to build. This amazing steel arch stands more than 600' (185 m) high, so its foundations go 60' (18 m) into the ground! It can be seen for 30 miles (48 km) in all directions. Hold the ends of a 9" (22.5) chain 3" (7.5 cm) apart and you'll see the arch's beautiful shape — upside down, of course!

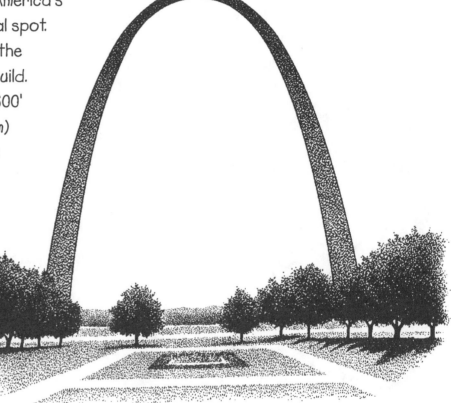

Dream it, Then Do it!

Build a mile-long bridge over rough waters and through wild winds? Impossible, they said. Joseph Strauss, the chief engineer of the Golden Gate Bridge (page 53) answered, "Don't be afraid to dream." Dreaming of something new takes imagination. Without American imagination we wouldn't have a Constitution (page 25), the automobile (page 81), or a soaring structure like the Gateway Arch (page 55).

Dreamers must be problem solvers too. Give it a try. Can you bridge a gap with paper?

❶ Set two stacks of books about 6" (15 cm) apart. Have several pieces of 4" x 11" (10 x 27.5 cm) paper handy.

❷ Set a flat sheet between the two stacks of books. Set a quarter on top. What happens?

❸ Now try folded or crumpled sheets. Or, roll and tape a sheet to make a "beam." Can you make the paper strong enough to support the quarter? Which way works best?

SEE IF A PAPER "BEAM" BETWEEN THE BOOKS WILL SUPPORT THE QUARTER.

This Land Is Your Land

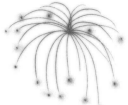

This Land Is Your Land

This land is your land

This land is my land

From California to the New York island

From the redwood forest, to the Gulf Stream waters

This land was made for you and me.

Woody Guthrie loved music and America. He spent much of his life roaming the country and writing more than 1,000 folk songs. This one is his best known. It tells about the beauty of our land and how all Americans can appreciate and enjoy it. Go rambling in your part of America. What do you see to sing about?

Wish You Were Here!

Discover the American treasures close to *your* home. Make postcards of these special places. Draw and label the site on one side of a large index card. Flip the card over and draw a line down the center. Ask a grown-up to help you write a few words about the site in the top left corner. Write a message to a friend on the left-hand side. Address and stamp the postcard on the right. You just might have folks from far away stopping by to see your special part of the U.S.A.!

Long Ago in America

Look out your window. Now close your eyes and imagine what you might have seen 50, or 100, or even 300 years ago. Would you see cars and tall buildings or *wickiups* (page 60) and open plains? Would you smell horsey smells, soot, or car exhaust? Would you hear clomping horses, clucking hens, or the honking of Model T cars?

Although there would be many changes, some things would stay the same. Americans have always longed for freedom. People always work hard to make the best lives for their families. And kids always love to play games and have fun!

Put yourself in America long ago. How would your life have been different — or the same? Explore unknown lands with your field log. Make a freedom drum. Parachute across enemy lines, and more. Learn America's amazing story by experiencing life way back when!

Early Native Americans

Imagine a world with no shopping malls, cars, or computers. That's how it was long ago, right where you live! Life was very different, but there were still wonderful communities. *Communities* are groups of people who help each other work, play, and live a good life.

We call these first people who lived in North America **Native Americans**. They weren't just one big group, however. There were many different tribes, each with its own language, traditions, and ways of living that depended on what the land and the weather were like where the tribe was located.

All of these self-reliant native peoples carefully used what they found around them to make homes, clothing, food, and even toys. They used their imaginations and what they found in nature to make the simple things they used each day become magnificent.

They told wondrous stories to pass along their history and created beautiful ceremonies to honor the earth. Today, Native Americans all over America keep many of these very special ancient ways alive.

Home, Sweet Home

★ ★ ★ ★ ★ ★ ★ ★ ★ ★ ★ ★ ★ ★ ★ ★ ★

You'd call it a *wigwam* if you lived in the east or near the Great Lakes. You'd call it a *wickiup* (WICK-ee-up) if you were a desert or plains dweller. These English words come from Indian words in two Native American languages. By any name, this structure is home when you're on the go.

How would you make it? First *saplings* (young trees) were bent into a dome-shaped frame. The frame was then covered with *soil*, small branches, animal hides, grass mats, bark and other natural materials. Here's a mini-home that you can make!

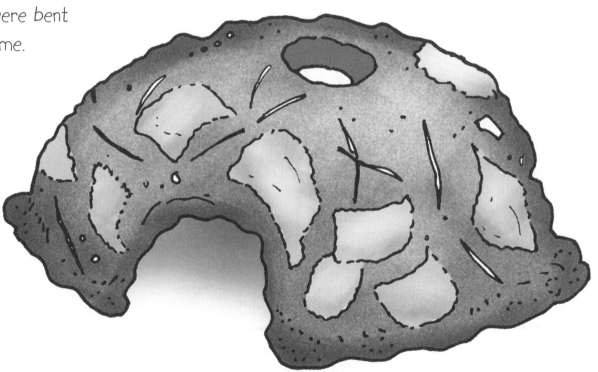

★★ You'll need ★★

2 small bowls
Plastic bag
1 cup (250 ml) fine dirt
½ cup (125 ml) flour
Grass, small leaves, and twigs
Scraps of brown paper bag

❶ Wrap one bowl in the plastic bag (to keep the mud from sticking). Set it upside down.

❷ In the other bowl, mix the dirt with the flour. Add enough water to make clay. Press the mixture onto the small bowl. Be sure to leave an opening to get inside and a hole in the roof for smoke from the cooking fire to escape.

❸ Press the grass, small leaves, and twigs into the mud.

❹ Wet the scraps of brown bag. Press them into the mud to look like hides.

❺ When the house is completely dry, carefully lift it off the bowl.

Navajo Bracelet

★ ★ ★ ★ ★ ★ ★ ★ ★ ★ ★ ★ ★

Turquoise is a blue-green stone found in the American Southwest. The Navajo people set the gem in silver. Sometimes jewelry was hammered and shaped from melted silver coins.

★ ★ You'll need ★ ★

Child safety scissors
Toilet-paper tube
Aluminum foil

Turquoise-colored paper
Glue

Shape Symmetry

The Navajo liked *symmetry* (both sides look the same). Try cutting some shapes from folded paper. When you unfold it, you'll have a *symmetrical* shape. They also liked animal shapes like lizards or butterflies.

❶ Cut a band from a toilet-paper tube. Cover it with foil.

❷ Cut shapes from the paper (see box).

❸ Glue the paper shapes onto the foil.

Your new turquoise bracelet might bring you health, happiness, and good luck. That's what the Navajo believed!

Play Toss and Count

Some Native Americans enjoyed playing games of luck. They tossed carved bone or antler playing pieces into a bowl or basket.

❶ Use a marker to decorate one side of six plum pits, dried beans, or almonds.

❷ Gather 20 twigs or pebbles for each player. Set them all in one pile.

❸ Place the pits on the lid of a plastic food container.

❹ To play, toss the pits into the air. You get a twig or pebble marker for each pit that lands decorated-side up.

Toss gently! Pits that land off the lid don't count.

❺ Take turns with your friends. When the twigs or pebbles are gone, each player counts her pebbles. The player with the most pebbles is the winner.

From 13 Colonies to a Nation

How's this for a family trip? You travel to a new land in a small ship. Expect storm after storm for months. You'll probably get sick. You'll definitely be cold, wet, dirty, and hungry. What's there to eat? Moldy cheese and hard biscuits. You'll likely find worms in your food. You finally arrive on land and hope your troubles are over. No way! It's time to build your home, grow food, find fresh water, and survive through a hard winter in an unfamiliar place.

Why would anyone say yes to this adventure? Hundreds of years ago people from England believed they could make a better life for themselves if they came to this New World called America. It was so important for them to believe and think in their own ways — something they couldn't do in England — that they were willing to make this dangerous journey to freedom.

People in the New World lived in *colonies*. That means they were still ruled by the King of England. It just didn't seem fair to people in America that they should have to obey a king, especially one so far away. It wasn't long before people began to think, "Let's rule ourselves!" And that's just what we Americans did. We became a new nation called the **United States of America**. We wrote the Declaration of Independence (page 22) to announce our freedom. Then we fought the **Revolutionary War** with England to win it!

Make Scrap Dolls

★ ★ ★ ★ ★ ★ ★ ★ ★ ★ ★ ★ ★ ★ ★ ★

In Colonial America, everything had to be made: homes, furniture, clothing, food ... everything! With so much to do and so few supplies, making toys for kids was the last thing people had time for. You could have a simple doll, if it was easy to make from things you could find. Nuts, balls of clay, or dried apples might form the head. Rags, cloth scraps, or cornhusks might form the body.

Make yourself a doll in the scrap-doll style using today's throwaway plastic grocery bags. Add a face with a permanent marker. Or, do what resourceful pioneer kids did. Just use your imagination to pretend your doll looks happy, sad, or sleepy.

★ ★ You'll need ★ ★

Child safety scissors
8 plastic grocery bags
Rubber bands

Permanent marker, optional

Make a doll with a skirt

❶ Cut the handles off one bag. Stuff another bag in the bottom of the first bag to form a head.

❷ Cut the handles from another bag. Roll it tightly into a log shape.

❸ Tie the log around the stuffed bag just below the head. The ends of the log form the arms. The rest of the bag forms a skirt.

USE RUBBER BAND HERE

USE RUBBER BAND ON THE LOG HERE

❹ Create hands by tying rubber bands at the ends of the arms.

Make a doll with legs

❶ Leaving the handles on the first bag, follow steps 1 through 4 on the left.

❷ Stuff a bag into the skirt to form a body.

❸ Roll another bag into a log shape. Join each log half and a handle together with a rubber band.

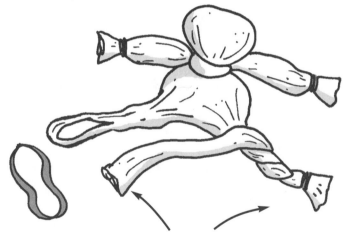

USE RUBBER BANDS TO JOIN LOG AND HANDLE

❹ Create feet with rubber bands at the ends of the legs.

Minutemen Relay

Minutemen *were dads, farmers, shopkeepers, and any other men willing to defend a Colonial village at "a minute's notice" during the Revolutionary War, America's war with England for independence. They had to be fast and work well together.*

Play this relay game to practice the speed and team spirit of the minutemen.

❶ On two large sheets of paper, draw circles for faces. Tape the sheets to a wall. Form two teams of about five kids. Stand in two lines across from the paper faces.

❷ Ready, set, go! Holding a marker, the first person in each team walks quickly to the paper and draws eyes in the circle. They walk back and hand the markers to the next kid in line. The first team to complete the eyes, nose, mouth, ears, hair, and hat of a minuteman is the winner!

It's a Crazy Mixed-Up World ...

... when a powerful country like England loses a war to a poor, new nation like the United States. Some say the British band played this British children's song called "The World Turned Upside Down" when they *surrendered* (gave up) to the Americans. The words go like this:

If buttercups buzzed after the bee,

If boats were on land, churches on sea,

If ponies rode men and grass ate the cows,

And cats should be chased to holes by the mouse,

If summer were spring and the other way round,

Then all the world would be upside down.

Hand Out Handbills!

People had many wonderful, new ideas during Colonial times. If you lived then, how could you quickly share ideas without e-mail or the phone? Use handbills! These messages were printed and then posted in places where lots of people would see them. Give it a try and see how it works!

Think. What would you like to say? Share a new idea? Invite friends to a meeting? Tell about something important that just happened? You decide!

Write. Use a black marker to write words and draw pictures on a sheet of white paper.

Copy. Make several photocopies.

Post. Tape the handbills (ask permission first) around your school or home. Post them on trees, doors, and walls for all to see. Now everyone knows about your event, meeting, or new idea!

The Lewis and Clark Expedition

In 1803, France owned a large section of land in the middle of what is now the United States. President Jefferson arranged for the United States to buy it in what's called the Louisiana Purchase. This new land doubled the size of our country. That wonderful — but wild and rugged — land was now part of America!

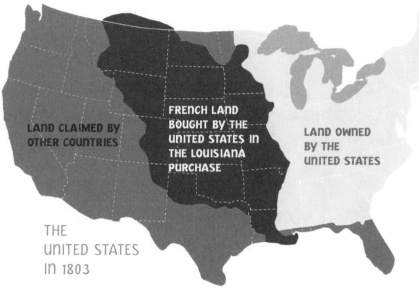

LAND CLAIMED BY OTHER COUNTRIES

FRENCH LAND BOUGHT BY THE UNITED STATES IN THE LOUISIANA PURCHASE

LAND OWNED BY THE UNITED STATES

THE UNITED STATES IN 1803

You are here, OK?

Jefferson sent a group of explorers, led by **Meriwether Lewis** and **William Clark**, to check it out. Along the route, many Native American tribes showed them the way and helped them on the difficult journey from St. Louis, Missouri, to the Pacific Ocean and back. The trip took almost 2½ years!

Make a Field Log

★ ★ ★ ★ ★ ★ ★ ★ ★ ★ ★ ★ ★

Put yourself back in time to 1803. It's your job to check out every detail of the land between St. Louis and the Pacific Ocean! What would be your most valuable piece of equipment on this 8,000-mile (12,872-km) journey? No, not a camera. There weren't any back then! Why, your trusty field log would be just right for sketching and writing notes about the land, plants, animals, and people you see along the way! And that's just what Lieutenant Clark used.

★ ★ **You'll need** ★ ★

Ruler
Pencil
Child safety scissors
Brown paper grocery bag
3 sheets of paper
Hole punch
2' (60 cm) of string or yarn

❶ Ask a grown-up to help you measure and cut a 9" x 12" (22.5 x 30 cm) rectangle from the grocery bag for the log's "leather hide" cover. If you want to make the paper look more like leather, wet it and crumple it up. Then flatten it and let it dry. Fold the short edges together.

❷ Stack the sheets of paper and fold them in half (top to bottom). Slip them inside the cover.

❸ Punch two holes near the fold.

Thread with yarn or string.

❹ Pretend you are exploring your backyard, park, or school-yard for the first time. You want to share its wonders with your friends back home. Sketch and label what you see in your field log. Draw birds, bugs, plants, rocks — anything and everything!

Thank you, Sacagawea!

Uh-oh, field logs overboard! That's what happened one windy day on the Lewis and Clark expedition. Luckily, **Sacagawea** was aboard the boat. As the water washed precious cargo into the river, this Shoshone Indian guide grabbed and saved whatever she could.

Sacagawea was a hero in other ways, too. She helped the explorers find food from the land. She helped them speak to and trade with different Native American tribes. Special gold dollars were made in 1997 with her picture to honor this brave woman.

Westward Ho!

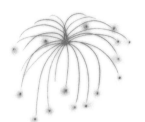
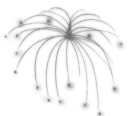

The Lewis and Clark expedition (page 69) opened up the western half of America. More trappers traveled west for valuable fur hides. Miners traveled west searching for gold.

Then, families like yours headed west looking for farmland and a better life. Imagine your parents telling you it was time to say good-bye to your friends and belongings. You would journey 2,000 miles (3,218 km) from your home.

You would face blizzards, steep cliffs, dangerous river crossings, and fierce grizzly bears. Once you arrived, there'd be no comfortable hotel where you could relax. Your first home might be a *dugout*, carved into the side of a hill. No fast-food burgers! You'd eat homegrown food. No superstores! Your clothes, blankets, and beds would be made from the flax, feathers, or wool from your farm. Are you ready to be a pioneer in a new land?

Are we there yet?

Tecumseh's Dream

> Sell a country! Why not sell the air, the clouds and the great sea, as well as the earth? Did not the Great Spirit make them all for the use of his children?

Pioneers traveled west across America, building homes and towns. But their new homes were on land where many different Native American tribes had lived for thousands of years. **Tecumseh** was a member of the Shawnee, a tribe in Ohio. He had a plan to save the homelands of the Native Americans. For years, he worked to unite tribes all over the Midwest and the West into one great nation. It took great courage to fight for the rights of the native peoples. Sadly, Tecumseh died in battle. He is remembered as one of the greatest leaders of the Shawnee.

Possibles Bag

★ ★ ★ ★ ★ ★ ★ ★ ★ ★ ★ ★

Call it a knapsack, a *poke sack* (a small cloth bag carried by soldiers in the Civil War, page 78), or a possibles bag, this special pouch to carry supplies is handy when you're on the move. Native Americans carried pouches. So did explorers, trappers, and pioneer kids moving west. A possibles bag was used to hold *possibles*, or personal items such as medicine, a lock of hair, or *flint* (a special stone for starting a fire). What special things will you carry in your "leather hide" bag?

★ ★ You'll need ★ ★

Ruler
Child safety scissors
Brown paper grocery bag
Paper clip
Hole punch
6' (2 m) of string or yarn
Glue

❶ Ask a grown-up to help you measure and cut three pieces out of the bag: 6" x 10" (15 x 25 cm), 6" x 6" (15 x 15 cm), and 3" x 6" (7.5 x 15 cm). If you want to make the paper pieces look more like leather, wet them and crumple them up. Then flatten them and let them dry.

❷ Place the paper square on the larger rectangle. Hold it in place with the paper clip as you punch holes around the edges.

❸ Thread the string or yarn in and out of the holes as shown. Tie the ends together to make a shoulder strap.

❹ Round off the corners of the large rectangle. Fold over to make a flap.

❺ Snip along one of the longer edges of the small rectangle to make fringe. Glue it between the front and back of the bag at the bottom.

Now decide what precious treasures go inside!

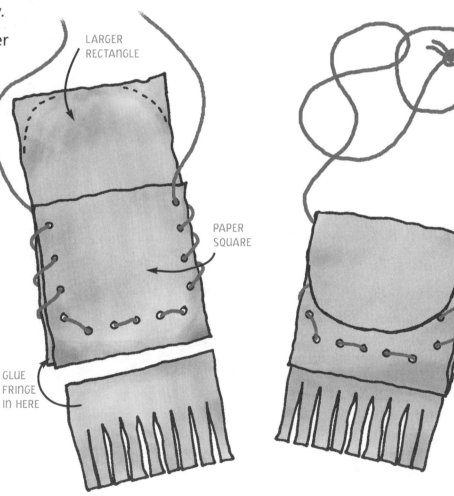

LARGER RECTANGLE

PAPER SQUARE

GLUE FRINGE IN HERE

Pioneer Movies

★ ★ ★ ★ ★ ★ ★ ★ ★ ★ ★ ★ ★

Shadow theaters were do-it-yourself movies, pioneer-style. A candle behind a hanging sheet made the screen. Cutout figures told the tales. What imaginative fun!

★ ★ You'll need ★ ★

Child safety scissors
Large cereal box
Tape
Sheet of white paper
Glue and paper scraps, optional
Markers
Drinking straws
Small rock or other weight
Flashlight and a partner to hold it

Make the screen

❶ Have a grown-up help you cut two windows in the large sides of the cereal box. Save the cardboard.

❷ Tape the sheet of paper over one window. Cover the frame with paper scraps to decorate it, if you like.

Make the puppets

❶ On the cutout cereal-box cardboard, draw people and animal characters. Cut them out.

❷ Tape each one onto a drinking straw.

Let it roll!

❶ Place the screen on the edge of the table. Set the rock in the bottom to hold it steady. Have your partner shine the flashlight on the screen. For the sharpest shadows, hold the puppets very close to the back of the screen.

❷ Retell a favorite story such as *The Gingerbread Man, The Three Billy Goats Gruff,* or *The Little Red Hen.* Tell a tale your grandparents have shared. Tell a tall tale.

BAWK!

America Divided

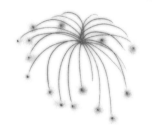

Imagine a time when America was split apart in many ways. While many people lived the American dream of freedom, many others did not. Black people in the South were not free. They were bought as slaves and forced to do hard work. Even kids like you picked cotton and did hard chores for long hours.

Many Americans, mostly from the northern states, thought that slavery was wrong and that the laws should be changed. The plantation owners in the southern states, who depended on the slaves' labor, wanted things to stay the way they were. It was such a big disagreement that most of the southern states separated from the North to form their own country.

In 1861, President Abraham Lincoln led America into the **Civil War** to keep our states united as one country. The war also freed the slaves. All Americans were reminded that liberty and justice is for all, no matter what color we are.

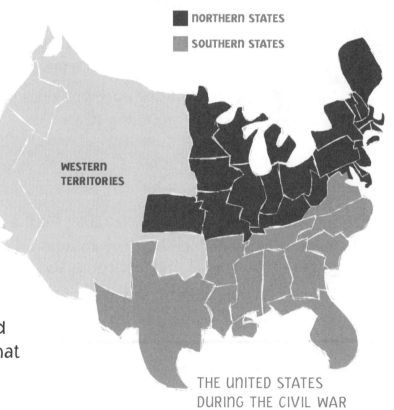

NORTHERN STATES
SOUTHERN STATES

WESTERN TERRITORIES

THE UNITED STATES DURING THE CIVIL WAR

Make a Freedom Drum

★ ★ ★ ★ ★ ★ ★ ★ ★ ★ ★ ★ ★ ★ ★ ★ ★ ★

Slaves made music to keep the hope of freedom alive. Singing made hard fieldwork easier to get through. Some songs and rhythms reminded slaves of their lives in Africa. Others were codes for escape. Drumbeats were sometimes used as a secret language.

Drumming sounds great in a group. Beat a rhythm on your drum with your hands. Repeat it a few times. Can your friends follow you on their drums? Take turns being drumbeat leader. Pass the beat from person to person like a message to be free.

★ ★ You'll need ★ ★

Child safety scissors
Brown paper grocery bag
Round ice-cream carton
Glue
Tan plastic grocery bag
Large rubber band

❶ Cut off one large side of the paper grocery bag. Wet and crumple it, then flatten it and let it dry.

❷ Ask a grown-up to help you cut it to the size of the ice-cream carton. Glue it to the outside. Now your carton looks like the hollowed logs slaves used to make drums.

❸ Slaves used an animal hide for the drumhead. Cut a hide shape from the plastic grocery bag. Hold it in place over the bottom of the carton with the rubber band.

The New Century

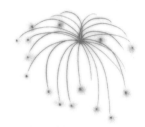

Welcome to 1900, a new century — and a world of new ideas and contraptions. Some people owned all the latest inventions: telephones, automobiles, electric lights. Others worked hard in the factories that made those new things. Some families were so poor that even children your age had to work to help out. See what life was like 100 years ago.

Henry Ford's Big Idea!

Imagine a time when cars were so expensive that few people could afford them. Then Henry Ford had an idea to produce more of them faster so they would be cheaper to buy. Here's how he might have explained it to the factory workers: "Let's use exactly the same parts to make every car. Let's have the car move along from worker to worker as it's being made. Let's have each worker repeat just one of the steps needed to build the car each time a car comes by."

Ford's new system worked! He broke all the car production and sales records at the time as millions of cars that families could afford rolled off his *assembly line*.

Let's hear it for the American imagination, which has brought us many great inventions!

Work on an Assembly Line

★ ★

Try it yourself. Build tops with your friends. Use all the same parts. Pass each top from kid to kid. Each kid does just one step. Go through the steps four times so that each kid has a finished top.

★ ★ You'll need ★ ★

4 bolts
8 washers that fit the bolts
4 old CDs
4 nuts
Masking tape

Kid #1: Load the bolt with a washer, a CD, and a washer, in that order.

Kid #2: Screw a nut onto the bolt until it's up against the washer to hold it all in place.

Kid #3: Tape around the top of the bolt for a smooth handle.

Kid #4: Test the top.

Life Is Changed Forever

What invention most changed life in America? Many think it was the car. By 1927, some 15 million of Henry Ford's Model T's jammed the roads. Think about how your family uses a car to:

- ★ Go to school
- ★ Shop for groceries
- ★ Get to work
- ★ See a movie
- ★ Visit relatives
- ★ Go on vacation

What else? Count how many car trips your family makes in one day. If you live in the city, does your family still own a car? How often do you use it? Now imagine how different life would be if you never used a car!

flick Pics

★ ★ ★ ★ ★ ★ ★ ★

Imagine this crazy contraption. Drop a nickel into a machine. Turn the crank and look through the viewer. You'll *see* a moving picture. Sure, it doesn't even last a minute, but wow, it looks *so* real! One hundred years ago, more than 1 million nickels a day were spent at *nickelodeons* just to *see* these amazing first movies. Try making your own instant movie!

★ ★ You'll need ★ ★

Markers
Index card (one for each "movie")
Drinking straw
Tape

Try These Ideas!

★ Frog, person, or bunny jumping
★ Bird's wings flapping up and down
★ Eyes opening and closing
★ Umbrella opening and closing

❶ Draw a different motion or action on each side of the index card. For example, you might draw a smiling face on one side and a sad face on the other side.

❷ Tape the card to the top of the straw.

❸ For action, roll the straw back and forth between your palms. Enjoy the show!

FRONT   BACK

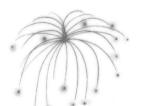
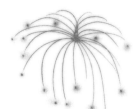

America in World War II

In the late 1930s, life was peaceful in America, but faraway in Europe, things were different. A cruel dictator and his friends were trying to conquer the world. What should Americans do? Some thought we should stay out of the war. After all, we were protected by two oceans. Others felt that with our deep love of freedom and self-rule, Americans must help our friends in other countries be free.

Then a surprise attack on an American naval base at **Pearl Harbor in Hawaii** made most Americans agree, our country must go to war! This war was called World War II ("World War Two") because it was the second time in the 1900s that so many countries and regions of the world were involved in the fighting. Millions of soldiers left to fight in Europe, Asia, and Africa. Americans did what they could at home to help. Times were hard, and many lives were lost. Americans showed we are willing to give our lives for the freedom of others around the world.

Make a Mini-Parachute

★ ★ ★ ★ ★ ★ ★ ★ ★ ★ ★ ★ ★ ★ ★ ★ ★

Parachutes were used to drop soldiers and supplies out of airplanes into enemy land. Parachutes even dropped *dummies* (stuffed figures that look like people) from airplanes just to trick the enemy. Experiment with your own mini-parachute to see how this enormous silk-and-rope contraption prevents a crash landing.

★ ★ You'll need ★ ★

Ruler
Marker
Child safety scissors
Plastic grocery bag
Thread
Tape
Jumbo paper clip
Index card

❶ Have a grown-up help you measure and cut a 12" (30 cm) square from the grocery bag.

❷ Cut four 12" (30 cm) lengths of thread. Tape one to each corner of the bag.

❸ Gather the free ends of the threads together and knot them. Slip one paper clip onto the knot.

❹ Cut the index card in half. Draw a picture of a soldier or supply chest on one side of the card. Clip it to the parachute.

❺ Pinch the center of the parachute. Toss it high into the air or down a staircase.

Drop a paper clip at the same time as your parachute. Which crash-lands? Which way would you prefer to travel?

Even Dogs Helped!

Would you volunteer your dog to help the soldiers? First of all, your dog must be big (at least 50 pounds/22.5 kg), young (1 to 5 years old), and smart! Dogs had to follow commands like "come," "stay," and *"heel"* (walk close by). They learned to crawl close to the ground to avoid flying bullets and being seen so they could deliver messages on the battlefield. Their powerful sense of smell and hearing made them awesome guards. And some even learned to parachute through the sky.

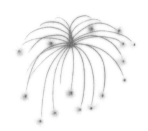
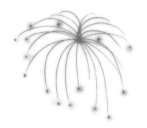

Make History!

History is the toys you play with, what you ate for lunch, and what you watched on TV last weekend. Your life will be history ... to your children, and your children's children, and to their children. Hang onto that history so you can pass it along! Preserve your family's traditions, memories, and special events (page 89). And while you're at it, record some valuable history from your parents as well as from your grand-parents and other older relatives, too (page 90).

Tradition Keeper

★ ★ ★ ★ ★ ★ ★ ★ ★ ★ ★ ★ ★ ★ ★ ★ ★

Traditions are things your family does in a special way every year, like having a big picnic on the Fourth of July, or breaking a piñata on your birthday, or eating moon cake at New Year's. Foods, songs, games, celebrations ... anything we do can become a tradition.

Make a special keeper to hold your family's traditions. Now you'll remember to pass these special ways of the *past* on to your own children who will live in the *future*.

★ ★ You'll need ★ ★

Child safety scissors
2 large paper plates
Markers
Hole punch
6' (2 m) of yarn
Index cards

❶ Have a grown-up help you cut the top halves of the plates into matching heart shapes.

❷ Decorate the hearts with markers. Add your family name or names.

❸ Punch matching holes around the bottom edges of both plates. Stitch them together. Tie the ends of the yarn into a bow for hanging.

❹ Write or draw a favorite family tradition on each index card. Store the cards in the keeper.

Blast from the Past

Interview your parents or grandparents about their past. You can record what they say with a tape recorder. Or, they might prefer to write down their memories. You can also write or draw what they tell you about. Try the questions below. Then think of more of your own.

★ What did you do for fun when you were a kid?

★ What was school like?

★ What were your favorite foods?

★ Did you use computers, CDs, or a television?

★ How did you travel?

★ Tell me about this old photo.

★ Sing a song from when you were a kid.

★ How has life changed? How is it the same?

Celebrate America!

What better way to honor the American spirit than with a celebration "from sea to shining sea"? National holidays and annual traditions bring us together to remember great people and events in American history and to reflect upon the qualities that make our nation strong.

When we fly the flag, share a Thanksgiving dinner, visit a memorial, or watch a parade, we show appreciation for the values that define our country: liberty, justice, tolerance, and appreciation for diversity. We honor those who, throughout history, have dedicated their lives to upholding these ideals. And we reflect upon the virtues that have shaped America — determination, imagination, leadership, courage, and hard work. Here are some new traditions to help you celebrate these special American days!

Thanksgiving Day

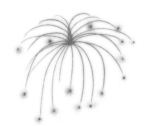
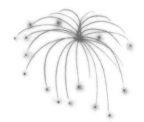

What could be better than a holiday feast with family and friends? That's what happens on **Thanksgiving**. It's nice to be thankful for delicious food, fun times, and each other, as we celebrate together.

Almost 400 years ago, early settlers called *Pilgrims* came to America from England. It was dangerous to sail across the Atlantic Ocean in their small ship, the *Mayflower*. It was tough to live through a terrible winter in an unfamiliar land. Without the help of the Wampanoag (wam-pa-nog), Native Americans living nearby, the Pilgrims would not have survived. After almost a year in the new land, it was time to party — and be *very* thankful! It was traditional for both the Native Americans and the English settlers to have a harvest celebration, so they gathered together to share a big feast. Today, we remember the Pilgrims and show appreciation for the native people who helped them with the special fall feast we now call Thanksgiving.

Mooooo...

Thanksgiving Day is celebrated on the fourth Thursday of November.

Mini-Mayflower

★ ★ ★ ★ ★ ★ ★ ★ ★ ★ ★ ★ ★ ★ ★

Sail your mini-Mayflower through the ocean as you think about the Pilgrims' long, dangerous voyage.

★ ★ You'll need ★ ★

Markers or crayons

White cardboard

Child safety scissors

Blue, gray, and brown construction paper

Glue

Index card

Tape

Piece of string or yarn at least twice as wide as your cardboard

Stapler

❶ Color sky at the top of the cardboard.

❷ Cut waves from a strip of the blue paper. Glue on the waves along the very bottom of the cardboard.

❸ Cut out a gray rock shape and a brown dock shape. Glue on these shapes, one at each end of the waves, and label them.

❹ Draw the *Mayflower* ship on the index card. Cut it out. Tape the string to the bottom of the ship.

❺ Slip the bottom of the ship behind the waves. Tie the string behind the cardboard.

❻ Staple the waves to the card above and below the string on both sides. Pull the string to make the *Mayflower* sail along.

So Thankful!

There was so much for the Pilgrims to be thankful for.

★ They had survived a long, dangerous voyage from England.
★ They had built homes to protect their families from the harsh winter.
★ The friendly native people had taught them how to grow food and hunt.

But most important, they could worship in their own way. The life they worked so hard to make for themselves had come true!

A Long Journey

Ask a grown-up for a calendar you can write on. Find September 16. That's the day in 1620 that the Pilgrims left Plymouth, England, for America. From September 16 on, draw waves in each square of the calendar. On November 19, draw a tree. That's the day they anchored off Cape Cod on the Massachusetts coast. Then, more waves until December 21. That's the day they made their famous landing. The Pilgrims settled on the Wampanoag homeland at Patuxet, which English explorers had renamed Plymouth.

Massasoit, A Wise Wampanoag Leader

The word *Wampanoag* means "eastern people" or "people of the first light." When the Pilgrims arrived, there were more than 60 Wampanoag villages scattered along the East Coast in what's now Massachusetts and Rhode Island.

Massasoit was the leader of a village called Sowams. *Massasoit*, which means "chief of chiefs," was a title of great respect. His real name was Ousamequin ("yellow feather"). In March of 1621, he signed a peace *treaty* (agreement) with the English and in the fall, he attended the harvest celebration with 90 other Wampanoag men. To this day, Massasoit is highly respected among his people as a wise and brave leader.

Cornucopia of Thanks

★ ★ ★ ★ ★ ★ ★ ★ ★ ★ ★

What are *you* thankful for? Share it in this colorful centerpiece!

★ ★ You'll need ★ ★

Large brown paper lunch bag

Fresh fruit

Fall leaves (if available)

Construction paper in fall leaf colors

Child safety scissors

Marker

Make the cornucopia

❶ Fold down the opening of the paper bag to form a cuff. Twist the other end to form a cone shape.

❷ Set the bag in the center of the dinner table. Place the fruit inside and in front of the cornucopia.

Make the leaves

❶ Trace or draw leaf shapes onto the construction paper. Cut them out.

❷ Have Thanksgiving guests write their names and the date on one side. On the other, they can write something for which they are thankful (*my family, our town library, my kitten …*).

❸ Scatter the leaves around the cornucopia.

Independence Day

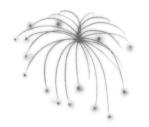

The "birth" of America began with an amazing announcement: We Americans are independent. We won't take orders from a faraway king of England. We will make up our own rules and pick our own leaders. We each have the equal right to live happily and freely. More than 200 years ago, it was incredible that ordinary people could be so powerful!

These ideas were written as the Declaration of Independence (page 22). Our leaders signed the paper on July 4, 1776. You know this day as **the Fourth of July**. Can you see why it's a joyful day of picnics, celebrations, parades, and fireworks?

Put on a Happy Birthday bash for our country — and your friends and family!

Independence Day is celebrated on the fourth of July.

HAPPY BIRTHDAY U.S.A.

CARA
HANNAH
Jon
Jamar
EMILY
JACOB
MAKAYLA

A Sparkling Invitation!

★ ★ ★ ★ ★ ★ ★ ★ ★ ★ ★ ★ ★ ★ ★ ★ ★

Let everyone know you're throwing
a big party!

★ ★ You'll need ★ ★

Sheet of white paper
Wax crayons
Paintbrush
Black watercolor paint
Glue
Glitter

❶ Fold the paper in half. On the front, draw stars and fireworks, pressing hard with wax crayons.

❷ Brush black watercolor paint over your picture. Now it looks like the night sky exploding with color!

❸ When dry, lightly spread glue on your fireworks and stars, and sprinkle on a little glitter so they really sparkle! Inside, write the time and place of your Independence Day bash!

Fireworks Party Hat

★ ★ ★ ★ ★ ★ ★ ★ ★ ★ ★ ★ ★ ★ ★ ★ ★ ★

Celebrate in style in this red, white, and blue birthday hat!

★ ★ You'll need ★ ★

Tape

White (2 sheets), blue, and red construction paper

Child safety scissors

Red marker

Glue

Red tempera paint

Paintbrush

Pencil

Make It Your Way!

You can also decorate your way. Here are some ideas:

★ Make some Snip Snap Stars (page 106) and glue them on the blue band or on the tips of the streamers.

★ Write "I (heart shape) U.S.A." on the band.

---

❶ Tape the short edges of the white paper together to make one long piece. Have a grown-up hold the hat around your head and tape the other short edges together so it's the right size.

❷ Cut a band of blue paper to fit across the front of the hat. Use a marker to write "Happy Birthday U.S.A.!" in big red letters across the band. Glue it onto the hat.

❸ Paint stripes of red from the top of the hat down to the band. Let dry.

❹ Cut strips of red paper. Roll them around a pencil to curl them. Tape them to the top edge of the hat. You look like a firework!

When in the Course of Human Events ...

Ask grown-ups to kick off the fun by reading some of the most famous lines from the Declaration of Independence (page 22). You'll find a copy online at the National Archives.

Just go to: **<http://www.archives.gov/national_archives_experience/declaration.html>**.

You can also see a photo of the original document! Sam Fink's book *The Declaration of Independence* also helps kids understand the words. Each phrase is illustrated with a helpful cartoon.

Now ring bells to honor the Liberty Bell's chime at the first reading of the Declaration (page 11) and let the party begin!

Firecracker Noisemaker

Push and vibrate the air with this gizmo to make a loud boom. Fold a sheet of newspaper in half and then fold as shown. Decorate it with red and blue markers.

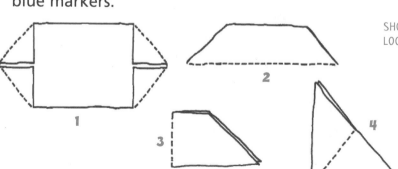

HOLD HERE

SHOULD LOOK LIKE THIS

BANG!

Patriotic Party Favors!

My Flag (page 7)

Balancing Bird (page 15)

Liberty Bell Pendant (page 12)

All-American Games!

Minutemen Relay (page 67)

Old Glory (page 101)

Play with the Presidents (page 110)

Fan-tastic Straw

Accordion-fold one fourth of a sheet of white paper. Open up the paper. Color every other fold red or blue. Refold and ask a grown-up to help you punch a hole in the center. Insert a drinking straw and tape in place as shown.

Eat Red, White, and Blue!

Dip a chip. Swirl white sour cream through red salsa. Serve with blue corn tortilla chips.

Patriotic parfait. Layer vanilla yogurt, ice cream, or pudding between layers of strawberries and blueberries. Serve in tall glasses.

July 4th coolers. Freeze blue and red sports drinks in ice-cube trays. You can also use raspberry and blueberry Kool-Aid. Serve the cubes in clear lemon-lime soda. Add a Fan-tastic Straw (above) and sip away.

Play Old Glory

All you need to play this game are 21 index cards, crayons (markers will bleed through), and three friends.

To make an all-American deck of cards:

Draw Old Glory, the American flag, on one index card. On the other cards, make 10 matching pairs of patriotic symbols. Here are some ideas:

★ Red star

★ White star

★ Blue star

★ Red stripes

★ Eagle

★ Liberty Bell

★ Liberty torch

★ U.S.A. in big letters

★ Fireworks

★ Your state's shape

❶ Deal the shuffled cards evenly among the four kids. Hold cards like a fan, blank side out.

❷ Take turns picking a card from the kid on your left. Lay down matching pairs as they are made.

❸ Continue until all cards are paired. The player left holding Old Glory is the winner!

Fourth of July Parade

Have everyone wear a Fireworks Party hat (page 98) and carry a Firecracker Noisemaker (page 99) and other Patriotic Party Favors (page 100). Now march to patriotic music like "You're a Grand Old Flag," "This Land Is Your Land," or "Yankee Doodle"!

July 4, 1788

Imagine this July 4 celebration in Philadelphia. Enough colonies had just agreed to the new Constitution (page 25), making the United States of America a true nation. Trumpeters led the parade. All-American floats from a huge eagle to an enormous Constitution to a real ship rolled through the city. And of course the rulers of this new nation, ordinary people, marched too. From carpenters to clock makers, from boatbuilders to bakers, folks of all trades stepped proudly to the beat of marching bands. At the end of the day, people rejoiced at a picnic — all 17,000 of them! Those folks really knew how to throw a party!

Flag Day

On June 14, 1777, our first leaders in the *Continental Congress,* our first government, made it clear that our new country needed a flag! So they approved a design.

"Resolved, that the Flag of the thirteen United States shall be thirteen stripes, alternate red and white; that the Union be thirteen stars, white on a blue field, representing a new constellation."

Although there are 50 stars for our 50 states on today's flag, it still displays stars and stripes in red, white, and blue. It's the number one symbol of America (see page 6).

Flag Day celebrates the birthday of our flag. On June 14 we show respect for our flag and country by displaying a flag in front of buildings.

Flag Day is celebrated on June 14.

BETSY ROSS

Stars and Stripes Wreath

★ ★

Here is a fun way to go all out for stars and stripes at your home!

★ ★ You'll need ★ ★

Child safety scissors
Paper plate
2' (60 cm) of yarn
White paper, optional
Red, white, and blue
    construction paper
Glue
Crepe paper or ribbon

❶ Ask a grown-up to help you cut the center from the paper plate, leaving a 2" (5 cm) rim.

❷ Pass the yarn through the plate and tie the ends together so you can hang it.

❸ Cut Snip Snap Stars (page 106), starting with a 4¼" x 5" (10.5 x 12.5 cm) piece of paper. Or, trace the stars on page 123 onto a piece of white paper and cut them out. Trace them to make more stars in red and blue. Glue them around the rim.

❹ Glue crepe-paper or ribbon streamers from the bottom. Hang proudly on your front door!

Star Spinner

★ ★ ★ ★ ★ ★ ★ ★ ★ ★

Watch this colorful star spin in the breeze! You can also make this spinner in the shape of an eagle (page 124), the Statue of Liberty's torch (page 20), or the Liberty Bell (page 123).

★ ★ **You'll need** ★ ★

Child safety scissors

Red, white, and blue paper

Glitter

Glue

Markers

Hole punch

String

Old CD

Tape

❶ Cut a Snip Snap Star (page 106) from colored paper. Decorate as you like with glitter, paper scraps, and markers. Punch a hole at the top and thread with a loop of the string for hanging.

❷ Trace around the CD on colored paper. Cut out the circle.

❸ Draw a spiral from the center of the circle to the edge.

❹ Cut along the line. Tape the center of the spiral to the bottom of the star.

Snip Snap Stars

Make five-pointed stars with one snip of your scissors! An 8½" x 10" (21 x 25 cm) piece of paper makes a nice big star. You can make other sizes, too. Just always keep the proportions of the paper you start with the same.

❶ Fold the paper in half.

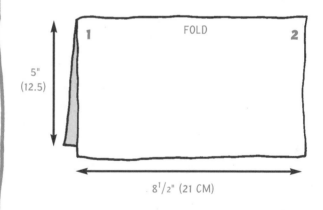

FOLD

1   2

5"
(12.5)

8¹/₂" (21 CM)

❷ Fold and unfold one way and then the other so you have fold lines that cross in the center.

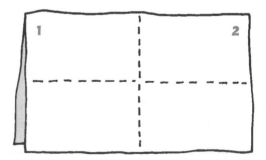

1   2

❸ Starting from the vertical fold line, bring corner 1 to meet the horizontal fold line.

FOLD FROM THE VERTICAL FOLD LINE

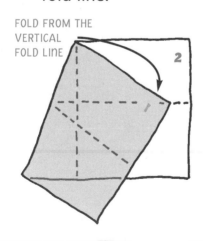

2

❹ Fold corner 1 back so that the edges line up.

❺ Fold corner 2 to the left.

❻ Fold corner 2 back to the right so that the edges line up.

❼ Now snip on the line shown. Open it up.

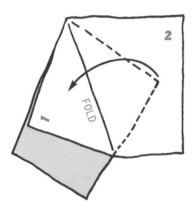

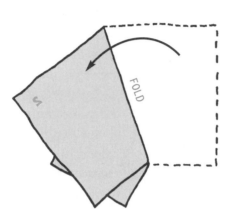

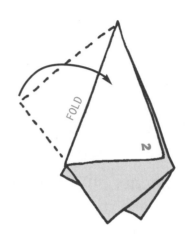

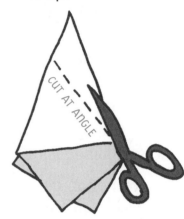

Wow, a perfect star!

Betsy's Star Shines!

There's a knock at the door. You open it and there stand three men, including General George Washington, head of the Continental Army! They ask if you'll sew the first American flag. They show you a sketch. They like your idea of making a five-pointed star (page 104) instead of their star with six points. What an honor! That's what some folks say happened to Betsy Ross in 1776!

Presidents' Day

Presidents' Day honors all past American presidents, especially George Washington and Abraham Lincoln. These men believed that the states on their own could not be as great as the states cooperating together. They truly believed in the *United* States of America, and they worked very hard to keep our states joined as one powerful nation.

We honor great presidents by placing their pictures on the coins we spend every day. You can remember these men by playing coin games on Presidents' Day.

Presidents' Day is celebrated on the third Monday in February.

Do you love to read books? That's what I loved to do when I was a kid. Being president was a big job. I led a fight to keep the states together as one nation. I thought slavery was wrong, so I put an end to it. Some people did not like my decisions. But I did what I knew was best for America. I made sure we stood by the important ideas our country was built on. That's what it takes to be a great leader.

Do you love math? I sure did. In fact, my first job was as a surveyor, measuring land. But I was most famous as "the father of our country." I led troops in winning a war for independence. Now we could build our own country. People had many different ideas how to do this. I said our country would fall apart if each state made its own rules. We needed to stay together to be strong. Many people liked what I did and thought. That's why I was elected the first president.

Play with the Presidents

These games challenge you to be as clever as a president!

PRESIDENT PICKUP

Setup: Place 10 coins in a row.

To play: Take turns with another player picking up coins. You may pick up one, two, or three coins on your turn. Don't be the player to pick up the last coin, or you lose!

ABRAHAM LINCOLN

LAST PRESIDENT LEFT

THOMAS JEFFERSON

Setup: Place three dimes in the top row, five nickels in the next row, and seven pennies in the bottom row.

To play: Take turns with another player picking up coins. You must pick up one or more coins from a single row on a turn. Be the player to pick up the last coin, and you win!

BLOCK THOSE PRESIDENTS!

Setup: On a sheet of paper, draw the game board shown here. One player has two pennies, the other has two nickels.

To play: Place your coins in the corners on the game board. Take turns moving a coin along a line to a new spot. Be the player to block the other player's coins from moving, and you win!

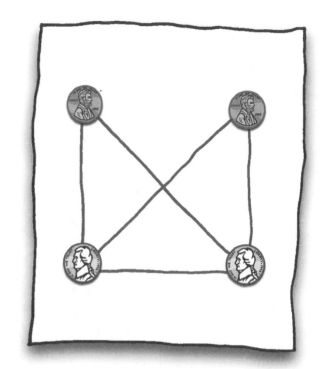

FRANKLIN DELANO ROOSEVELT

GEORGE WASHINGTON

Veterans Day and Memorial Day

On **Veterans Day**, we honor people who serve America in the U.S. armed forces (the Army, Navy, Marines, Air Force, and Coast Guard). On **Memorial Day**, we remember those who gave their lives for our country. How do we celebrate and show respect? Fly a flag. Visit a memorial. Place flowers and flags on graves. Listen to a speech or patriotic music. Watch a parade. And here are some other extra-special ways to show your appreciation and respect!

Veterans Day is November 11. Memorial Day is traditionally May 30 but is also celebrated on the last Monday in May.

Send a Message!

People in the armed forces always appreciate hearing from the folks back home. You can send an e-mail message to someone in the military at these websites:

<anyservicemember.navy.mil/MessageSend.html>

or

<www.underthestarsandstripes.com/troops.php>.

Dear Service Member,
I just wanted to let you know
how much I appreciate
what you're doing...

Flag Flyer

★ ★ ★ ★ ★ ★ ★ ★ ★

Hang this colorful Flag Flyer by your front door!

★ ★ You'll need ★ ★

Child safety scissors
Red and white
  construction paper
White paper, optional
Glue

Sheet of blue paper,
  11" x 17" (27.5 x 42.5 cm)
Red and white crepe paper
Hole punch
String

❶ Cut many star shapes out of the red and white paper. You can trace the star patterns on page 123 onto the white paper and use them to cut out more stars or cut Snip Snap Stars (page 106). Glue them onto the blue paper.

❷ Cut several 2' (60 cm) red and white crepe streamers. Glue them across the bottom edge.

❸ Glue the short edges of the paper together to make a tube.

❹ Punch two holes at the top of the tube. Thread a piece of the string through the holes. Knot the ends together.

❺ Hang your flyer outside in the breeze!

Sparkly Service Star

★ ★ ★ ★ ★ ★ ★ ★ ★ ★ ★ ★ ★ ★ ★ ★ ★

Hang one of these crystal-covered stars in your window for each family member in the military.

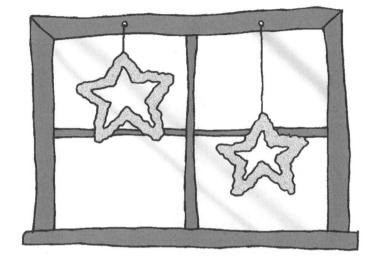

★ ★ You'll need ★ ★

Cup of boiling water
(for grown-up use only)
Heat-proof jar
3 tablespoons (45 ml) of Borax
Spoon
Blue pipe cleaner
String
Pencil

❶ Ask a grown-up to pour the boiling water into the jar.

❷ Mix in the Borax. Stir until the powder disappears.

❸ Shape the blue pipe cleaner into a star. Tie one end of the string to the star and the other to the pencil. Set the pencil on top of the jar, letting the star dangle in the water. Let it set overnight.

❹ When the star is covered with sparkly crystals, carefully lift it from the jar. Slip it off the pencil and hang it in a window.

A Monumental Contest

THIS SMALL SECTION OF THE ACTUAL WALL SHOWS JUST A FEW OF THE THOUSANDS OF NAMES INSCRIBED ON IT.

How do you build a great monument to the U.S. soldiers who fought in the Vietnam War? Hold a contest to find the best design! That's how the Wall of Names at the **Vietnam Veterans Memorial** came to be. Who would have thought that the winner would be a young college student, Maya Ying Lin? Her idea was simple, yet so powerful.

A V-shaped wall of polished black stone rises from the ground. It is engraved with the names of the more than 57,000 Americans who lost their lives in the war or who remain missing. Some people come to find the names of loved ones. Some leave flowers and mementos behind. Others take home rubbings of engraved names. No wonder it's the most visited monument in America.

Labor Day

Some of the heroes we admire we see on TV and in magazines. Others are part of our daily lives. These are community helpers who make America great. Firefighters, police officers, teachers, doctors, nurses, construction workers, office workers, and so many others work hard to keep us safe, smart, healthy, and happy.

To show our appreciation, on **Labor Day** we give working people a day off. Folks often spend time with friends and family enjoying the last days of outdoor summer fun! Some cities and communities have parades, and government officials make public speeches to honor workers' contributions.

Labor Day is celebrated on the first Monday in September.

THANK YOU!

I Can Be a ...

★ ★ ★ ★ ★ ★ ★ ★ ★ ★

Pick your favorite community helper and act out the part!

★ ★ You'll need ★ ★

Glue

Photo of your face (about 1"/2.5 cm in diameter)

Large index card

Markers

Child safety scissors

Tape

Drinking straw

Sheet of white paper

Paper clips

Cereal box

Make the "what I'll be" puppet

Think about which community helper you want to be when you grow up. Glue your photo-face near the top of the index card. Use the markers to add a hat and other clothing you'll wear. Cut yourself out. Tape the straw to the top back.

Make the "where I'll work" scene

On the sheet of paper, draw a scene showing where you'll work. Clip the paper to the top flap of the cereal box.

Go to work

Hold your puppet in front of the scene. Tell a story about your day at work.

Who Am I?

Give three clues about your job. Let others ask yes or no questions until they think they know and are ready to guess. Take turns. Here are some to get you started:

I mostly work outside. I help plants grow. What I make feeds people. *(farmer)*

I work inside. I help people learn. You can take home what I take care of but you'll need a special card. *(librarian)*

You might not see me, but you will see what I make. It is delicious! *(chef)*

Career Charades

Act out the job of a community helper. Can your friends guess the job? Take turns acting and guessing.

Community Helper ABC

Think of a job that starts with each letter of the alphabet like, **X**-ray technician, **y**ard worker, and **z**ookeeper. Now draw each worker on one sheet of paper. Put them together to make a book. Try this in your classroom, with each student making one or two pages.

Martin Luther King Jr. Day

Imagine not being able to drink from a fountain because your skin was a darker color than another person's. There was a time when black kids could not go to the same school as white kids. African Americans had to give up their seats on buses so that white people could sit down. They had to eat at different restaurants and swim in different pools.

Dr. Martin Luther King, Jr. knew this was not right, especially in America where, in the powerful words of the Declaration of Independence (page 22), "all men are created equal."

Dr. King taught through peaceful marches and powerful speeches that even if we look different from one another, we must still respect each other. Because of his leadership, people's minds changed and then laws were changed to protect the rights of all Americans.

January 15 is Dr. King's birthday. It's a day to serve your community in honor of this brave man's work for peace and equal rights. See ‹**www.mlk.org**› for ideas for your family and your school.

Dr. Martin Luther King Jr.'s birthday is celebrated on the third Monday in January.

Brotherhood Chain

★ ★ ★ ★ ★ ★ ★ ★ ★ ★ ★ ★ ★ ★

Hang this paper chain as a declaration of brotherhood and a reminder of Dr. King's dream of a peaceful world where we all get along with one another. How about a brotherhood chain for your classroom?

★ ★ You'll need ★ ★

Pencil

White paper

Child safety scissors

Tan and brown construction paper

Crayons or markers

Scraps of brightly colored paper

Glue

❶ Trace the person pattern shown on page 124 onto the white paper. Cut it out.

❷ Fold a piece of the construction paper in half. Place your cutout on the construction paper, against the fold. Trace the cutout.

❸ Cut out the construction-paper person and unfold it. Decorate the person with the crayons or markers and paper scraps to look like you. Make many more to look like your friends.

❹ Cut strips of the brightly colored paper.

❺ To assemble the chain, glue each paper person's hands together. Glue the strips into loops that connect each person.

friendship Light catcher

★ ★

Make this light catcher with a friend. Then hang it in a window to let sunlight sparkle through your friendship shapes!

★ ★ You'll need ★ ★

Marker

Friend

Paper

Crayons

Salad oil

Cotton ball

Child safety scissors

Tape

❶ With the marker, trace your friend's hand on the paper.

❷ Place your hand so it overlaps the outline and let your friend trace your hand.

❸ Color with your friend. Color in the shapes made where the lines cross. Press hard with crayons. Leave some areas uncolored.

❹ Put oil on the cotton ball. Rub the design.

❺ Cut it out. Tape it to a window.

THINK ABOUT IT!

Can you think of ways to keep Dr. King's message of fairness and brotherhood alive?

What is *your* dream for America?

Rosa Parks Takes a Stand

On a December evening in 1955, Rosa Parks took the bus home after a long day at work. She sat down. Suddenly the driver asked Rosa to give up her seat. Why? Her skin was black, and a white man wanted to sit down. That was the law at that time in Montgomery, Alabama, and in other parts of America, too. Rosa knew the law was unfair. So she refused to move! The police came and took her to jail.

Many people heard about brave Rosa Parks. Organized by Dr. King (page 118) and other black leaders, thousands of people refused to ride the city buses for almost a year. Finally, the Supreme Court (the most powerful court in America) ruled that the law went against the rights guaranteed by the U.S. Constitution (page 25), and so it was changed. Rosa Parks, Dr. King, and many other courageous people worked hard for fair treatment and equality for all!

One-Child Classroom

In the fall of 1960 in New Orleans, Louisiana, **Ruby Bridges** was the only child in her first-grade classroom. Why? Because her skin was dark, white parents did not want their kids to learn alongside her, so Ruby learned alone. Every day she came to school, people shouted mean words and shook their fists at her. So *U.S. Marshals* (special law enforcement officials) had to protect her. Ruby never gave up. Thanks to Ruby — and to the many other brave African American students in places like Little Rock, Arkansas — the public schools were *integrated*. Now kids of all skin colors come to school together across America.

From Many, One!

Get a magnifying glass and a dollar bill. Have a grown-up help you to read the tiny words on the ribbon in the eagle's beak: *E Pluribus Unum*. Those Latin words mean "from many, one." They first reminded Americans that from many colonies came one great nation (page 64). Remember that our money is a symbol (page 5) of our country. What powerful message do those words send today? From many people comes one great nation!

What Makes America So Awesome?

Our people, of course! America's greatness comes from our dreams and ideas, and what we do to make them happen.

From people of many countries, religions, ideas, and customs, we have become one great nation! In America, we understand that it's the diversity of our people that makes our country rich with wonderful ideas. We are different from each other, but we are still one nation, America …

with liberty and justice for all!

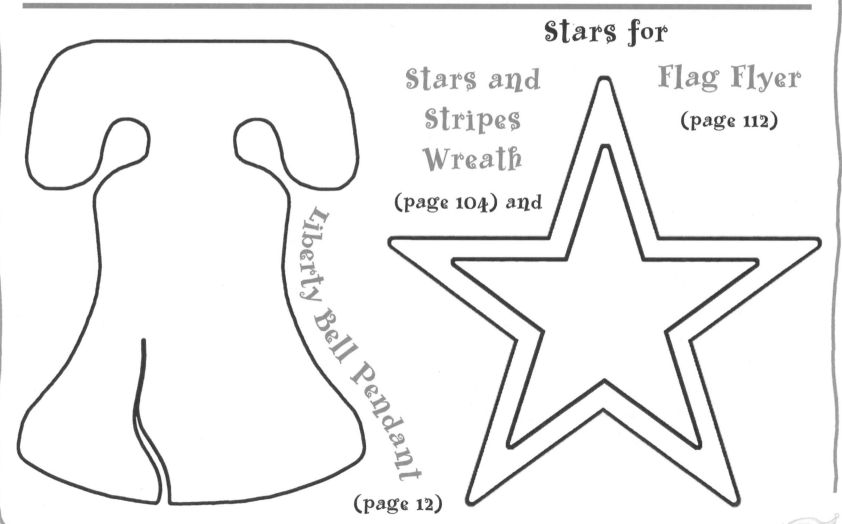

Liberty Bell Pendant

(page 12)

Stars and
Stripes
Wreath

(page 104) and

Stars for

Flag Flyer

(page 112)

Balancing Bird
(page 15)

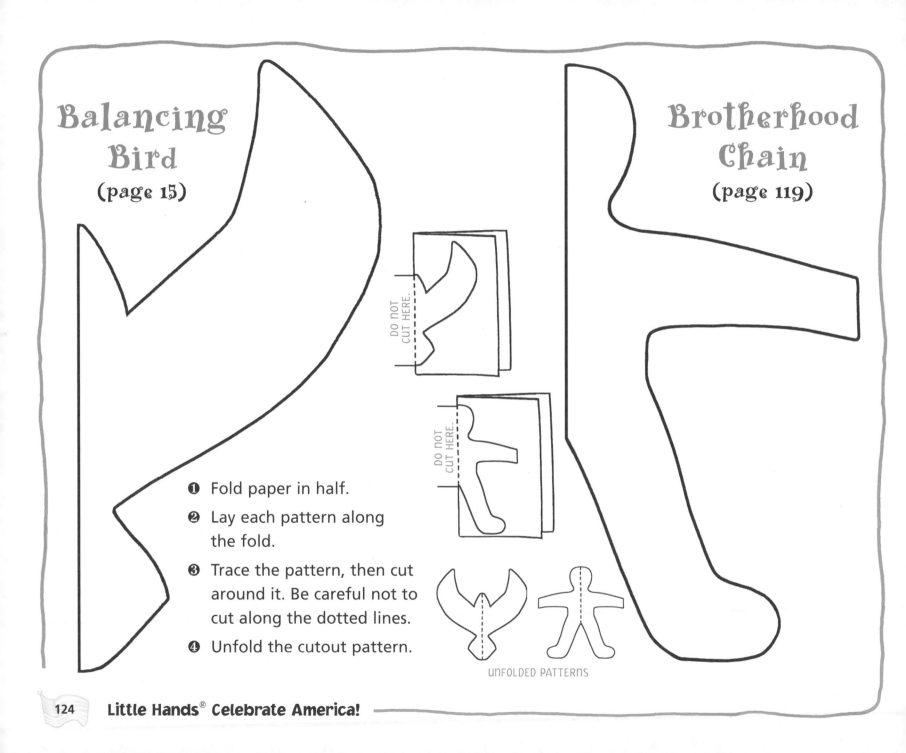

Brotherhood Chain
(page 119)

DO NOT CUT HERE.

DO NOT CUT HERE.

❶ Fold paper in half.

❷ Lay each pattern along the fold.

❸ Trace the pattern, then cut around it. Be careful not to cut along the dotted lines.

❹ Unfold the cutout pattern.

UNFOLDED PATTERNS

Index

More Good Books from Williamson Publishing

  Other Williamson Books by Jill Frankel Hauser

Parents' Choice Recommended
EASY ART FUN!
Do-It-Yourself Crafts for Beginning Readers
A *Little Hands®* book for ages 3 to 7, $12.95

WOW! I'M READING!
Fun Activities to Make Reading Happen
A *Little Hands®* book for ages 3 to 7, $12.95

American Institute of Physics Science Writing Award
Early Childhood News Directors' Choice Award
SCIENCE PLAY!
Beginning Discoveries for 2- to 6-Year-Olds
A *Little Hands®* book for ages 2 to 6, $12.95

American Bookseller Pick of the Lists
Dr. Toy Best Vacation Product
KIDS' CRAZY ART CONCOCTIONS
50 Mysterious Mixtures for Art & Craft Fun
A Williamson *Kids Can!®* book for ages 7 to 14, $12.95

Parents' Choice Honor Award
American Institute of Physics Science Writing Award
GIZMOS & GADGETS
Creating Science Contraptions that Work
  (& Knowing Why)
A Williamson *Kids Can!®* book for ages 7 to 14, $12.95

American Bookseller Pick of the Lists
Benjamin Franklin Best Juvenile Nonfiction Award
SUPER SCIENCE CONCOCTIONS
50 Mysterious Mixtures for Fabulous Fun
A Williamson *Kids Can!®* book for ages 7 to 14, $12.95

 Williamson's *Little Hands®* Books

Little Hands® books for ages 2 to 7 are 128 to 160 pages, fully illustrated, trade paper, 10 x 8, $12.95 US/$19.95 CAN.

Little Hands®
SEA LIFE ART & ACTIVITIES
Creative Learning Experiences
  for 3- to 7-Year-Olds
by Judy Press

Little Hands®
EARLY LEARNING SKILL-BUILDERS
Colors, Shapes, Numbers & Letters
by Mary Tomczyk

ALL AROUND TOWN
Exploring Your Community Through Craft Fun
by Judy Press

Parents' Choice Recommended
AT THE ZOO!
Explore the Animal World with Craft Fun
by Judy Press

AROUND-THE-WORLD ART & ACTIVITIES
Visiting the 7 Continents Through Craft Fun
by Judy Press

Parents' Guide Classic Award
Real Life Award
The Little Hands ART BOOK
Exploring Arts & Crafts with 2- to 6-Year-Olds
by Judy Press

Parents' Choice Approved
Little Hands®
FINGERPLAYS & ACTION SONGS
Seasonal Rhymes & Creative Play for
  2- to 6-Year-Olds
by Emily Stetson and Vicky Congdon

Parents' Choice Approved
Little Hands® **PAPER PLATE CRAFTS**
Creative Art Fun for 3- to 7-Year-Olds
by Laura Check

ARTSTARTS for Little Hands!
Fun Discoveries for 3- to 7-Year-Olds
by Judy Press

The Little Hands PLAYTIME! Book
50 Activities to Encourage Cooperation
  & Sharing
by Regina Curtis

Parent's Guide Children's Media Award
ALPHABET ART
With A to Z Animal Art & Fingerplays
by Judy Press

MATH PLAY!
80 Ways to Count & Learn
by Diane McGowan and Mark
  Schrooten

American Bookseller Pick of the Lists
RAINY DAY PLAY!
Explore, Create, Discover, Pretend
by Nancy Fusco Castaldo

Parents' Choice Gold Award
FUN WITH MY 5 SENSES
Activities to Build Learning Readiness
by Sarah A. Williamson

Parents' Choice Approved
The Little Hands BIG FUN CRAFT BOOK
Creative Fun for 2- to 6-Year-Olds
by Judy Press

Parents' Choice Approved
The Little Hands NATURE BOOK
Earth, Sky, Critters & More
by Nancy Fusco Castaldo

And More ...

Parents Magazine Parents' Pick
KIDS LEARN AMERICA!
Bringing Geography to Life with People,
    Places & History
by Patricia Gordon and Reed C. Snow
A **Williamson** *Kids Can!*® book for ages
    7 to 14, $12.95 US/$19.95 CAN

Children's Book Council Notable Social Studies
    Trade Book
WHO *REALLY* DISCOVERED AMERICA?
Unraveling the Mystery & Solving the Puzzle
by Avery Hart
A *Kaleidoscope Kids*® book for ages 7 to 14,
    $12.95 US/$19.95 CAN

Selection of Book-of-the-Month; Scholastic Book Clubs
KIDS COOK!
Fabulous Food for the Whole Family
by Sarah Williamson and Zachary Williamson
A **Williamson** *Kids Can!*® book for ages 7 and older,
    $12.95 US/$19.95 CAN

Parents' Choice Gold Award
Benjamin Franklin Best Juvenile Nonfiction Award
KIDS MAKE MUSIC!
Clapping and Tapping from Bach to Rock
by Avery Hart and Paul Mantell
A **Williamson** *Kids Can!*® book for ages 6 to 14,
    $12.95 US/$19.95 CAN

HANDS AROUND THE WORLD
365 Creative Ways to Build Cultural Awareness
    & Global Respect
by Susan Milord
A **Williamson** *Kids Can!*® book for ages 6 to 14,
    $12.95 US/$19.95 CAN

KIDS' EASY BIKE CARE
Tune-Ups, Tools & Quick Fixes
by Steve Cole
A *Quick Starts for Kids!*® book for ages 8 and older,
    $8.95 US/$10.95 CAN

Dr. Toy 100 Best Children's Products
Dr. Toy 10 Best Socially Responsible Products
MAKE YOUR OWN BIRDHOUSES & FEEDERS
by Robyn Haus
A *Quick Starts for Kids!*® book for ages 8 and older,
    $8.95 US/$10.95 CAN

Parents' Choice Approved
Benjamin Franklin Best Multicultural Book Award
TALES OF THE SHIMMERING SKY
Ten Global Folktales with Activities
by Susan Milord
A *Tales Alive!*® book, full-color original art,
    $14.95 US/$23.95 CAN

Parents' Choice Honor Award
Benjamin Franklin Best Juvenile Fiction Award
TALES ALIVE!
Ten Multicultural Folktales with Activities
by Susan Milord
A *Tales Alive!*® book, full-color original art,
    $14.95 US/$23.95 CAN

Visit Our Website!

To see what's new at Williamson and learn more about specific books, visit our website at:

www.williamsonbooks.com

To Order Books:

Williamson Books
535 Metroplex Drive, Suite 250
Nashville, Tennessee 37211

The toll-free phone number and fax are:

    phone: 1-800-586-2572
    fax: 1-888-815-2759